National Fo

Scenic
Byways
East & South

Beverly Magley

FALCON®

HELENA, MONTANA

A FALCON GUIDE®

Falcon® Publishing is continually expanding its list of recreational guide-books. All books include detailed descriptions, accurate maps, and all the information necessary for enjoyable trips. You can order extra copies of this book and get information and prices for other Falcon® guidebooks by writing Falcon, P.O. Box 1718, Helena, MT 59624, or by calling toll-free 1-800-582-2665. Also, please ask for a free copy of our current catalog. Visit our website at www.FalconOutdoors.com or contact us by e-mail at falcon@falcon.com.

CAUTION
Outdoor recreational activities are by their very nature potentially hazard-ous. All participants in such activities must assume the responsibility for their own actions and safety. The information contained in this guidebook cannot replace sound judgment and good decision-making skills, which help reduce risk exposure, nor does the scope of this book allow for disclo-sure of all the potential hazards and risks involved in such activities.

Learn as much as possible about the outdoor recreational activities in which you participate, prepare for the unexpected, and be cautious. The reward is a safer and more enjoyable experience.

♻ Text pages printed on recycled paper

*To my father, who inspired an enduring
love of travel and interest in the natural world,
and to my mother, whose ability to stretch a dollar
made family travel possible.*

Contents

Foreword

Driving for pleasure is the most popular form of outdoor recreation in America and the most often chosen activity of the millions of visitors to the National Forests each year. These Forests—156 of them in 44 states—offer a wide array of outdoor recreation opportunity from camping and hiking to boating and bird watching. All this and more is offered amid the breathtaking splendor of the natural beauty of our nation. Now the Forest Service has developed a system of Scenic Byways to help you explore and enjoy America's Great Outdoors—our National Forests!

Forest Service employees are proud to be the managers and caretakers of these lands. Along with the natural resources upon which this country has come to depend, we are eager to share the story of the rich cultural, historical, and geological heritage the National Forests offer our visitors. From Alaska on the Pacific to Florida on the Atlantic, these byways offer some 3,000 miles of driving pleasure in 28 states.

Catch the fever of the gold rush days along Oregon's Blue Mountain Scenic Byway or encounter the drama of a Tennessee Civil War battlefield on the nation's first Scenic Byway, Ocoee—U.S. Highway 64. Experience the vast arid desert of New Mexico, enjoy the painted finery of fall colors in New Hampshire or visit the swamps and savannahs of Florida—all along the National Forest Scenic Byways.

Whether you are an armchair traveler or an on-site visitor, you may use this book to learn more about the Scenic Byways and the National Forests through which they wander. However you travel, we especially invite you to learn about and become involved in the management and care of your National Forests. We invite you to join us in enjoying the National Forests—America's Great Outdoors.

—F. Dale Robertson, former Chief, USDA Forest Service

Acknowledgments

This author could not have custom-designed a more enjoyable way to spend time than writing and editing this guidebook. I wish to thank the many people with the USDA Forest Service who spent hours giving me, and the other writers, valuable and insightful information about the scenic byways, and who then proofed the final write-ups for accuracy. This book reflects the dedication and genuine interest of Forest Service rangers and employees who shared their knowledge so willingly.

Sincere thanks to the writers and photographers who contributed byway descriptions and photographs. It was a pleasure to work with them and to learn about the scenic byways in their regions.

Last, but not least, the support of family and friends is essential and was freely given. I am grateful.

—Beverly Magley

Partners in Scenic Byways

The national forest scenic byways program has benefited from a unique partnership between the Plymouth Division of Chrysler Corporation and the Forest Education Foundation. This partnership represents a new era of cooperation between government and the private sector to promote recreation on public lands.

The Forest Education Foundation is a non-profit educational foundation chartered to raise funds through public donations and commercial sector grants. Funds are disbursed through program grants to support worthy projects, primarily in the area of recreation on public lands.

The Foundation engineered the partnership between the Forest Service and Plymouth and administers several key elements of the Scenic Byways program.

Plymouth recognizes the critical role passenger cars play in the enjoyment of America's scenic roads. Plymouth has designated the National Forest Scenic Byways program as a major focus in its efforts to operate as an environmentally conscious and responsible corporate citizen.

Plymouth supports national promotion of the scenic byways and provides funds for byways' signage, turnouts, and site improvements in the forest. The Plymouth exhibit promoting national forest scenic byways visitation travels the length and breadth of America each year.

Plymouth has also funded production of the scenic byways brochure for the Forest Service.

The Forest Education Foundation, Plymouth, and the Forest Service demonstrate how working together can enhance the recreational opportunities for all Americans.

For more information about Plymouth's sponsorship of the scenic byways program, please see your local Plymouth dealer. For information about the Forest Education Foundation, contact the Forest Education Foundation, P.O. Box 25469, Anaheim, CA 92825-5469, phone (714) 634-1050.

Introduction

The most popular form of outdoor recreation in our national forests is scenic driving. In response to this enjoyable pastime, the Forest Service established the national forest scenic byways program in May 1988.

Across the nation, national forest employees were invited to select their favorite roads, and their choices were wonderful. These spectacular routes take visitors alongside trout-filled streams, through diverse hardwood forests, over 13,000-foot passes, and to high alpine meadows, peaceful lakes, far-ranging views, cypress swamps, and much more.

There are 137 National Forest Scenic Byways scattered across the United States. Described in this book are the byways in the eastern half of the nation, some of the most beautiful and interesting places in the country. The eastern and southern byways cover more than 1,300 miles in 22 states, from Minnesota to Florida. Each is described in detail in this book.

Americans often think of national parks when planning a vacation, but national forests are the foremost providers of outdoor recreation in the country. Americans visit national forests twice as often as they visit national parks.

One reason is that national forests are usually much more accessible. There are 156 national forests in 44 states, covering a total of 8.5 percent of the United States. Most Americans live within a day's drive of one or more national forests.

Another reason is that national forests have so much to offer. About half of the nation's big game animals reside on national forests, along with a wide variety of other animals and plants, including rare and endangered species. These lands also contain 329 wilderness areas, 99,468 miles of trails, more than 6,000 campgrounds and picnic areas, more than 1,100 boating sites, and 307 winter sports areas.

In addition to traveling through magnificent countryside, national forest scenic byways provide access to varied recreational activities. Visitors can simply enjoy the scenery from the car. Or they can get out and meander along interpretive nature walks, picnic at a scenic overlook, boat on the many lakes and rivers, camp in secluded sites, or hike into wilderness areas for days or weeks.

Byway travel is educational. Through brochures, interpretive displays, visitor centers, and their own experiences, byway travelers have many opportunities to learn about natural history, human history, archaeology, geology, and national forest management, to name just a few subjects.

The byways are as varied as the landscape. Zilpo Road winds 9 miles across forested ridges to a lovely lake in eastern Kentucky, while the San Juan Skyway travels 236 miles through southwest Colorado's highest, most

The Ohio River Scenic Byway winds through Hoosier National Forest. DAVE KISSEL PHOTO

rugged peaks. Apalachee Savannahs Scenic Byway offers visitors to Florida's pine forest an opportunity to see odd, insect-eating pitcher plants and Venus flytraps, while Cascade Lakes Highway in Oregon provides great fishing and outstanding views of volcanic peaks. Travelers on Montana's Wise River–Polaris Road can dig for crystals in the Pioneer Mountains, while motorists in Arizona's Kaibab Plateau-North Rim Parkway end their route overlooking the Grand Canyon.

This new program is an exciting way people and businesses can form productive partnerships with the Forest Service. Various community organizations, volunteers, and national and local businesses are helping with the byway program. Their efforts in the next few years will make your trip more pleasurable and enlightening, as such facilities as interpretive signs, paved overlooks, and hiking trails are installed. In this way, the scenic byways program not only invites us to visit the national forests; it provides opportunities to get involved in conservation.

Whether you seek solitude or active participation, enjoy the national forest scenic byways.

How To Use This Book

National Forest Scenic Byways describes fifty byways all across the United States with maps, photos, and informative text.

Each byway description features a travel map that shows the byway, campgrounds, special features such as visitor centers and recreation areas, connecting roads, and nearby towns. Each map also displays a mileage scale and a state map that shows the general location of the byway. All byways are marked on the map on page 9. A legend to map symbols appears on page 8.

Each text description is divided into ten categories. Most are self-explanatory, but the following information may help you get the most from each description:

General description provides a quick summary of the length, location, and scenic features of the byway.

Special attractions are prominent and interesting activities and natural features found on the byway. Additional attractions are included in the description. Some activities, such as fishing and hunting, require permits or licenses that must be obtained locally.

Location gives the name of the national forest and the general area of the state in which the byway is located. It also describes exactly where the scenic byway designation begins and ends. The road numbers are normally

Along the Oscar Wiggington Memorial Scenic Byway in South Carolina. LARRY CRIBB PHOTO

found on a state highway map and are posted along the route. Occasionally, the scenic byways are on back roads that are not numbered on the state highway maps. In that case, the map of the byway includes primary routes from a nearby city or primary highway.

Byway route numbers are the specific highway numbers on which the scenic byway travels, such as U.S. Highway 12, or Arkansas Route 23, or Forest Road 1243.

Travel season notes if the byway is open year-round or closed seasonally. Many byways are closed to automobiles in winter, due to snow cover, but are delightful for snowshoeing, cross-country skiing, and snowmobiling. Opening and closing dates are approximate and subject to regional weather variations. Always check for local conditions.

Camping on the national forests can be a rich and varied experience. Services basic to all developed national forest campgrounds along the byway are listed in this category. Individual national forest campground names and their additional services or features are noted in the narrative. Many campgrounds charge a fee, noted at the campground entrance. National forest campgrounds generally provide the basics: toilets, picnic tables, and fire grates. Drinking water and garbage pickup are found at some. Electrical, water, and sewer hookups are rare.

Primitive dispersed camping is permitted at all national forests, subject to local and special restrictions. Check with the individual national forest for details.

Selected campsites may be reserved on some national forests, through the computerized reservation system. Call 1-800-280-2267 for campsite availability information. A fee is charged for the service.

Privately owned campgrounds, usually with full hookups, showers, and other amenities, are often located near the byways. Check with the local Chamber of Commerce for details.

Services list communities with at least a restaurant, groceries, lodging, phone, and gasoline. When a community has each of the services, but perhaps only one motel and a small cafe, it is noted as having services with limited availability.

Nearby attractions are major features or activities found within about fifty miles of the byway. Many of these make an interesting side trip and can be combined with byway travel.

The maps in this book cover each byway thoroughly. However, if you plan to take side trips or explore the area further, a Forest Service map is invaluable and can be obtained at all national forest offices for a small fee.

The drive description provides detailed traveler information, along with interesting regional history, geology, and natural history. Attractions are presented in the order a traveler encounters them when driving the route in

Black bears are often residents of the forests that National Forest Scenic Byways cross.
CHRISTOPHER CAUBLE PHOTO

the described direction. If you travel the route from the opposite direction, simply refer to the end of the byway descriptions first.

The appendix lists the names, addresses, and phone numbers of the national forest(s) for each scenic byway. The supervisor's office is first, followed by ranger districts. Travelers may wish to contact the district rangers for detailed area maps and information on specific subjects.

Scenic Byway Signs

Look for these distinctive road signs along every national forest scenic byway. Each byway is marked with the basic scenic byway sign, shown below, and some of these signs will carry a plate with the name of that byway. The smaller "blaze" sign will appear as a reminder sign along the route. The signs are in color—purple mountains, dark green trees and lettering, and pale, bluish-green foreground.

Map Legend

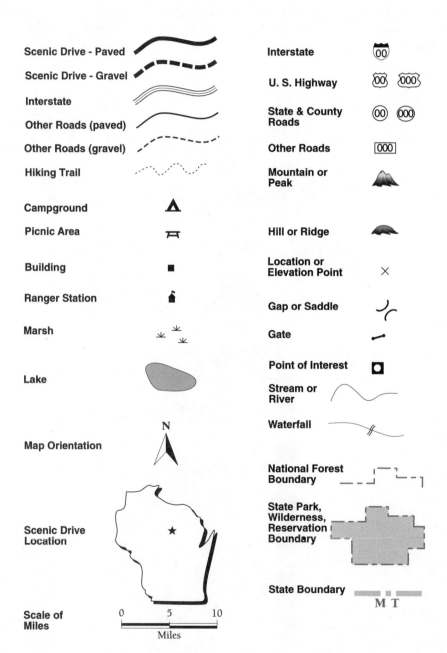

Scenic Drive - Paved

Scenic Drive - Gravel

Interstate

Other Roads (paved)

Other Roads (gravel)

Hiking Trail

Campground

Picnic Area

Building

Ranger Station

Marsh

Lake

Map Orientation

N

Scenic Drive Location

Scale of Miles

Interstate

U. S. Highway

State & County Roads

Other Roads

Mountain or Peak

Hill or Ridge

Location or Elevation Point

Gap or Saddle

Gate

Point of Interest

Stream or River

Waterfall

National Forest Boundary

State Park, Wilderness, Reservation Boundary

State Boundary

M T

Locations of the Scenic Byways

East

MAINE
Augusta

4

1 2 3
MINNESOTA
St. Paul

7   8
5   6
WISCONSIN

Madison

9

MICHIGAN
Lansing

Montpelier   18
VT
Concord
NH
Boston
MASS
Albany   Hartford Providence
NEW YORK   CONN

IOWA
Des Moines

ILLINOIS   Indianapolis   OHIO
INDIANA

Columbus   15

PENNSYLVANIA   Trenton
Harrisburg   NJ
Dover
MD.   Annapolis
Washington D.C.   DE

Jefferson
City   Springfield

MISSOURI

10   Frankfort

Charleston

11   KENTUCKY

WV   16
22   21   20   19

Richmond
VIRGINIA

12 13   14

Nashville   24   26
TENNESSEE   23   25

Raleigh
NORTH
CAROLINA

37 36 35
38 39
34

Little Rock

40
ARKANSAS

32

28   29   27
SOUTH
Columbia
CAROLINA
Atlanta

33

Jackson

31
Montgomery   GEORGIA
ALABAMA

South

Baton Rouge
LOUISIANA

30   Tallahassee

FLORIDA

1

Scenic Highway

Chippewa National Forest

General description: A 28-mile paved route through country rich in wetlands, forests, farms, and lakes.

Special attractions: Blackduck Lookout Tower, wildlife viewing, camping, boating, fishing, and hunting.

Location: North-central Minnesota in Chippewa National Forest.

Byway route numbers: Beltrami County Road 39 and Cass County Road 10.

Travel season: Year-round.

Camping: Three national forest campgrounds with picnic tables, fire grates, toilets, and drinking water.

Services: All traveler services, with limited availability, in Blackduck, Pennington, and Cass Lake.

Nearby attractions: Avenue of Pines scenic byway, ski areas, resorts, Turtle River canoe route.

For more information: See the appendix for contact information.

 The Drive

Scenic Highway provides a pleasant route between agricultural lands and forests. The two-lane paved route has narrow shoulders, and traffic is usually light. The traffic picks up a bit in mid-May at the start of walleye season.

Summer daytime temperatures are generally in the 80s to 90s. Insects can be annoying at times and you may want repellent. Spring and autumn are cooler and often wet, with days in the 50s and 60s and evenings in the 30s and 40s. Winter is nearly always below freezing.

The byway is scenic driven from either direction. When traveling north to south begin in Blackduck, where you may collect additional national forest information at the ranger station. Nearby, Blackduck Lake has camping, picnic areas, great walleye fishing, and a boat ramp.

Drive south on Beltrami County Road 39, through gently rolling farmland. A barrier-free fishing pier is provided at Gilstad Lake. A few miles south, Benjamin Lake has a nice sand beach for swimming and a pleasant picnic area in the hardwoods. Trees include basswood, birch, and maple.

Nearby, four buildings of historic Camp Rabideau Civilian Conservation

Drive 1: Scenic Highway
Chippewa National Forest

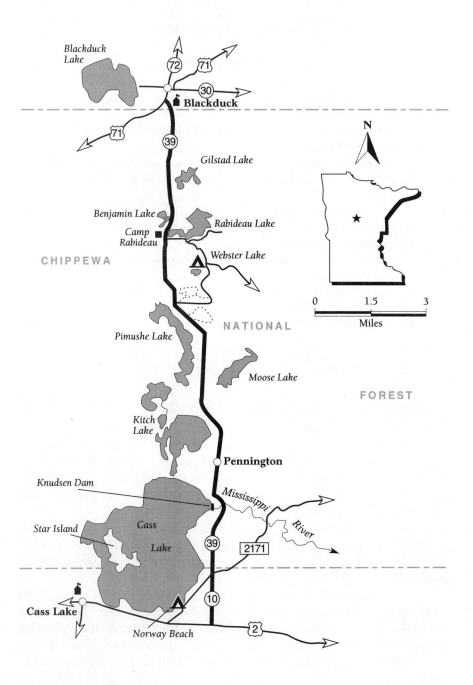

Blackduck Lake

72 71 30

Blackduck

71

39

Gilstad Lake

Benjamin Lake

Camp Rabideau

Rabideau Lake

CHIPPEWA

Webster Lake

N

NATIONAL

0   1.5   3
Miles

Pimushe Lake

Moose Lake

FOREST

Kitch Lake

Pennington

Knudsen Dam

Mississippi

Star Island

Cass Lake

River

39

2171

10

Cass Lake

Norway Beach

2

Corps (CCC) have been restored and are open for visitation in the summer. The camp was built in 1935, and CCC workers were housed there for the next five years. They planted thousands of trees, built the Blackduck Ranger District and two fire towers, counted deer, and performed numerous other tasks. Today, you can sample history by walking the one-mile interpretive trail through the camp.

Continue driving south on the byway through a beautiful forest of white and red pine intermixed with leafy quaking aspen, paper birch, Burr oak, and sugar and red maple. Autumn colors on this byway are lovely. Creeks and rivers provide openings in the forest, and you can glimpse black spruce bogs and expansive wetlands occupied by great blue herons, loons, a variety of ducks, and songbirds. Watch overhead for soaring bald eagles. The Chippewa National Forest has the highest concentration of breeding pairs in the lower 48 with 160 pairs of these endangered creatures. The number of breeding pairs has grown steadily every year, from 20 in 1963, to the present population. Another threatened animal, the gray wolf, is making a gradual comeback. An estimated 100 wolves live in the national forest, mostly north of U.S. Highway 2.

Webster Lake is just off the byway to the east. The campground is located on a shady, sandy ridge overlooking the lake. Swimming is pleasant

White sand invites swimmers to Norway Beach along Scenic Highway.
CHIPPEWA NATIONAL FOREST PHOTO

here. The adjacent picnic area is situated in a birch grove and has five tables and some fire rings. A hiking trail with a boardwalk through a bog encircles Webster Lake.

The byway continues through a corridor of trees and passes cabins, homes, and a few resorts. Pennington Bog is a Scientific Natural Area home to rare native orchids. You must have a permit to enter.

South of Pennington, the trees are predominately jack pine, quaking aspen, and paper birch. The byway shares the road with the Great River Road, a nationally designated route following the Mississippi River from its headwaters to the Gulf of Mexico. You'll cross the Mississippi River, which has more species of freshwater fish than any other river on our continent. Stop at Knutson Dam for great fishing (barrier-free access), picnicking, and camping. The area is full of both prehistoric and historic Indian artifacts, including a Paleolithic encampment complete with huge bison bones.

A few miles south at the county line, the highway changes numbers, from Beltrami County Road 39 to Cass County Road 10. Norway Beach has an interpretive center, ranger-led summer programs, four campgrounds, a lovely white sand beach, and hiking trails. The interpretive center is housed in Norway Beach Lodge, built of red pine logs in the early 1930s by the CCC. You can rent a boat and go to Star Island, unique because it has little lake of its own—a lake within a lake. Chief Yellowhead and the Ojibwe had villages on Star Island and near the Knutson Dam area. About two-thirds of the Chippewa National Forest is currently located on reservation lands.

The byway ends at the junction of U.S. Highway 2 and Cass County Road 10. Big old white pines lean over the road, their tops misshapen from years of wind. From here you could drive east to Deer River and the Avenue of Pines National Forest Scenic Byway.

2

Avenue of Pines Scenic Byway

Chippewa National Forest

General description: A 39-mile paved highway through extensive forests of red pine; past northern lakes, broad grassy meadows and wetlands, and several historic Indian sites.

Special attractions: Cut Foot Sioux Lake, Cut Foot Experimental Forest, Laurentian Divide, lakes, resorts, fishing, hiking, mountain biking, horseback riding, camping, snowmobiling, and cross-country skiing.

Location: North-central Minnesota on the Chippewa National Forest. The byway travels Minnesota State Highway 46 on national forest lands between Deer River and Northome.

Byway route number: Minnesota State Highway 46.

Travel season: Year-round.

Camping: Seven national forest campgrounds, with picnic tables, fire grates, drinking water, and toilets.

Services: Groceries, gas, and lodging with limited availability at Squaw Lake and Deer River. All traveler services available in nearby Grand Rapids.

Nearby attractions: Scenic Highway and Northwoods national forest scenic byways, state parks, downhill ski areas.

For more information: See the appendix for contact information.

 The Drive

The Avenue of Pines scenic byway travels through low-rolling hills covered in pine forests and lakes. The two-lane highway is paved and has narrow shoulders and frequent pullouts. Traffic is generally light. There are numerous private campgrounds with full hookups.

Summer daytime temperatures in northern Minnesota are generally in the 80s to 90s. Insects can be annoying at times and you may want repellent. Spring and autumn are cooler and often wet, with days in the 50s to 60s and evenings in the 30s and 40s. Winter is nearly always below freezing.

When driving the byway from south to north, you may wish to visit the Deer River Ranger District office to collect additional national forest information and maps or during the summer visit the Cut Foot Sioux Visitor Information Center in the middle of the scenic byway.

Drive 2: Avenue of Pines Scenic Byway
Chippewa National Forest

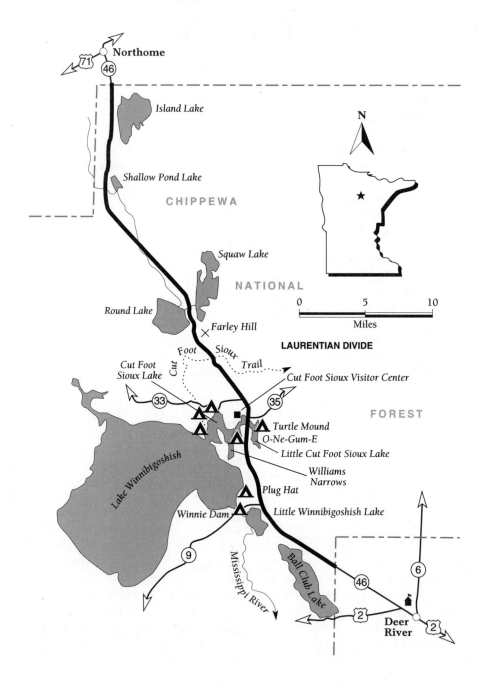

From Deer River, drive 1 mile west on U.S. Highway 2, then turn north on Minnesota State Highway 46. The scenic byway begins at the national forest boundary about 6 miles from Deer River and travels through relatively flat countryside, where agricultural fields are intermixed with forest. In the uplands, stands of red pine, aspen, birch, and fir dominate, while black spruce, tamarack, and cedar grow in the lowlands.

The Winnie Dam Corps of Engineers campground is located right below the dam, where the Mississippi River pours out of Lake Winnibigoshish. Winnie Dam was built in 1884. The campsites are located in a cool forest of red and white pines, and some sites have electric hookups. A trailer dumping station is provided. Boaters can launch into the Mississippi River and on into Little Winnibigoshish Lake.

Nearby, Plug Hat Point Campground (open only in springtime) sits in a grove of mature pines, oaks, and aspen on a small bluff above the lake. Several of the 12 sites overlook the lake, and a boat launch provides access to Little Winnibigoshish Lake.

North of Winnie Dam, the scenic byway enters the corridor of red pines, also known as Norway pines. The Civilian Conservation Corps (CCC) planted many of these trees in the 1930s. The corridor, or avenue of pines, becomes increasingly dense as you drive north.

Williams Narrows Campground's 17 sites sit in a shady stand of mature red and white pine, with a few Burr and red oak, and red maple. Some of the campsites overlook the lake. O-Ne-Gum-e Campground is in a similar woodland setting, with 46 sites. Some sites are barrier-free, and a few overlook Little Cut Foot Sioux Lake. There are additional campgrounds on the west side of Little Cut Foot Sioux Lake.

The Cut Foot Sioux area is a focal point for this scenic byway. Cut Foot Sioux is named for a warrior slain in 1748 in a battle between the Chippewa and the Sioux. A summer visitor information center has displays, a bookstore, and evening naturalist programs. A historic ranger station, listed in the National Register of Historic Places, is the oldest remaining station building in the Forest Service's eastern region. You may arrange a tour at the visitor center.

Good hiking trails are scattered throughout this area. Simpson Creek Trail has some shorter loops in its 13-mile length. The 22-mile Cut Foot Sioux Trail is a National Recreation Trail that meanders through this beautiful lakes and forests country and traverses the Laurentian Divide, the geographical high ground separating waters north to Hudson Bay or south to the Gulf of Mexico.

A few miles north of the visitor's center, motorists can take a 20-mile loop side trip on paved and gravel roads. The Cut Foot Sioux Scenic Drive

Avenue of Pines cuts a straight swath through a forest of big red pines.
CHIPPEWA NATIONAL FOREST PHOTO

leads through the forest to campgrounds, beautiful lake views, and wildlife observation points. A brochure is available at the visitor center.

Continuing north on the byway, Farley Hill Lookout is in the heart of the Cut Foot Experimental Forest. This old fire tower is built on an esker, a high point in the otherwise flat region. An esker is a geologic formation left by receding glaciers. You can't climb the old tower, but take a hike on a portion of the Cut Foot Sioux National Recreation Trail. If you choose to hike west, you'll hike through the forest past several beautiful little lakes. In the fall you can enjoy munching on wild blueberries or gathering wild hazelnuts from the bushes.

Typical wildlife seen in this region includes bald eagles, white-tailed deer, black bears, and beavers. Bird-watchers find more than 230 species of birds on the Chippewa National Forest. Look for crossbills, ruffed grouse, woodcock, broad-winged hawk, red-eyed vireo, and white-throated sparrow. The Chippewa National Forest has the highest concentration of breeding eagles in the lower 48—160 pairs. Look for them on the Mississippi River and around Winnibigoshish and Cass lakes.

This stretch of highway gives the scenic byway its name, Avenue of the Pines. The big red pines stretch in all directions and give a feeling of expansiveness to the forest. Pull off the road and walk through the shady understory of this beautiful, open forest.

The Indian community of Squaw Lake has a long history. Native Americans came here for hundreds of years to harvest the wild rice that nearly covers nearby Squaw Lake. The village has all traveler services, available on a limited basis. Round and Squaw lakes both have excellent walleye fisheries.

North of Round Lake, the scenery opens up more and the route travels over low-rolling hills and wetlands. Aspen, birch, and balsam fir mix with farms and fields of hay. You may be lucky enough to spot a shy timber wolf some evening.

Island Lake offers good fishing. The Elmwood Island Trail System provides a nice place to stretch your legs after riding in a boat.

The byway ends at the national forest boundary and the road continues to Northome, a small community that provides all traveler services—available on a limited basis.

3

Edge of the Wilderness Scenic Byway

Chippewa National Forest

General description: A 47-mile paved road through hardwood forests and along numerous lakes.

Special attractions: Suomi Hills and Trout Lake semi-primitive areas, Rice River Canoe Route, autumn colors, lakes, boating, fishing, camping, hiking, cross-country skiing, snowmobiling, historic sites.

Location: North-central Minnesota on the Chippewa National Forest. The byway is located within national forest boundaries on Minnesota State Highway 38, between Grand Rapids and Bigfork.

Byway route number: Minnesota State Highway 38.

Travel season: Year-round.

Camping: One national forest campground, with picnic tables, fire grates, toilets, drinking water.

Services: All traveler services in Grand Rapids. Limited services in Marcell, Effie, and Bigfork.

Nearby attractions: Avenue of Pines scenic byway, Big Fork River, numerous lakes, Scenic State Park, historic Iron Range, Iron World.

For more information: See the appendix for contact information.

 The Drive

Set in a region of hardwood forests and freshwater lakes, Northwoods Scenic Byway travels 22 miles along the edge of two beautiful semi-primitive areas. The two-lane highway is paved, with narrow shoulders and limited pullouts. A good portion has no passing lanes and traffic is light and generally slow because of the rolling, winding route.

Summer daytime temperatures are generally in the 80s to 90s. Insects can be annoying at times and you may want repellent. Spring and autumn are cooler and often wet, with days in the 50s to 60s and evenings in the 30s and 40s. Winter is nearly always below freezing and this byway gets a great deal of snow.

Driving north to south, begin in Bigfork. To the west, the Bigfork River is very scenic, with excellent canoeing, fishing, and boating opportunities. The Rice River Canoe Route begins in Marcell and travels 19 miles of river and lakes between Bigfork and Marcell.

Drive 3: Edge of the Wilderness Scenic Byway
Chippewa National Forest

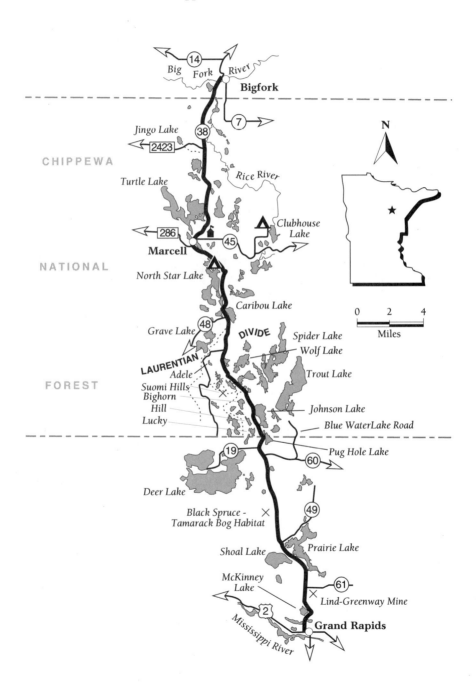

The byway parallels much of the old "Gut and Liver" railroad route between Bigfork and the national forest boundary north of Grand Rapids. Now the railroad bed is a groomed snowmobile trail with many optional loops and side trips along the route.

The byway travels south on Minnesota State Highway 38, through rolling terrain. White spruce, red pine, jack pine, paper birch, and tamarack surround lowland wetlands and meadows. This is a hilly region, where lakes are cradled by glacial moraine from the last Ice Age. The Chippewa National Forest has more than 700 lakes, 920 miles of streams, and 150,000 acres of wetlands. The Jingo Lake walking trail leads 5 miles through this pretty, rolling area. You could also take a short side trip east for good fishing in Johnson Lake.

Clubhouse Campground is about 7 miles east of Marcell, situated on the lake in a stand of 200-year-old red pine trees. There are 48 sites, a nice sandy swim beach, and a boat launch.

Marcell has a small store, motel, restaurants, and gas. Area activities are posted on the township's park kiosk. The Marcell Ranger District office has additional national forest information, such as brochures for The Chippewa Adventure, a 17.5-mile self-guided auto tour that loops east out of Marcell and travels the lakes and resort country, or the Fall Color Tour, 36 miles of brilliant autumn colors. With a Chippewa National Forest map, you can also design your own off-the-beaten-path loop on the many side roads along the byway. It's wise to check road conditions with the ranger first.

Watchable wildlife includes white-tailed deer, black bears, ruffed grouse, bald eagles, and numerous species of geese and ducks. The first stop on the Chippewa Adventure points out an osprey nest built on top of a dead tree. Another stop shows you super canopy white pine, which are virgin 200-year-old trees that stand well above the rest of the forest. These huge trees are used frequently by bald eagles for nesting and perching.

The Forest Service has ongoing projects to enhance trumpeter swan habitat. In the mid-1980s one pair established themselves on the Chippewa National Forest and they are one of just a few breeding pairs in Minnesota.

The landscape south of Marcell is very pretty. You'll get glimpses of lakes, surrounded by tree-covered hills. Hardwoods begin to dominate the forest south of Marcell. The white bark of quaking aspens and paper birch attract your eye, and sugar maples and red oaks add variety. Autumn colors can be breathtaking.

North Star Campground overlooks the lake and has some barrier-free sites. Aspens and other hardwoods are beginning to revegetate the area, which has a swimming beach and 38 campsites.

A few miles south, the byway crosses the Laurentian Divide and a

The Edge of the Wilderness Scenic Byway winds along numerous lakes in forested terrain.
CHIPPEWA NATIONAL FOREST PHOTO

pullout with restrooms, picnic tables, and an interpretive trail. A sign explains this geographic high point determines whether streams and rivers run north to Hudson Bay or south into the Gulf of Mexico.

Continuing south on the byway, the Suomi Hills Semiprimitive Nonmotorized Area lies 9 miles south of Marcell, west of the scenic byway. These 6,000 acres provide 21 miles of trails among the hills and lakes for nonmotorized travel only. Visitors come to camp, hike, mountain bike, canoe, cross-country ski, and bird watch. Try fishing for bass and panfish in Hill, Big Horn, Spruce Island, and Adele lakes. Lucky and Kremer lakes are stocked with trout. Just south of Day Lake, you can choose from several loop trails west of the highway. These hikes meander through the forest and bring you to beautiful backcountry lakes, including Spruce Island and Adele.

East of the byway, Trout Lake Semiprimitive Nonmotorized Area protects 4,500 acres of forest and lakes. Watch for loons, great blue herons, and occasional bald eagles. Gray wolves and coyotes also move through here. You can hike about 3 miles to Trout Lake, which is beautiful and very cold, with good fishing. The historic Joyce Estate was built on the southwest corner of the lake and provides a look at life in another era. Timber baron David Joyce built 30 buildings for his private hunting camp/summer home and included a golf course and shooting range. Today, you can walk through the big log lodge and stroll the grounds. The USDA Forest Service plans to restore the main lodge and two of the guest cabins. There are opportunities for dispersed primitive camping around the lake. To reach the trailhead, turn east on Itasca County Road 60, then north on Itasca County Road 335. Park at the locked gate and walk in.

The national forest boundary is in the birch and aspens along Pug Hole Lake. This is a pretty place for a picnic. A few miles east of Minnesota State Highway 38, you can park and hike 3 miles to Joyce Estate and Trout Lake.

Continue south on the byway to County Road 61 and the Lind-Greenway Mine. A trek on the Taconite Trail will provide an eye-opening view of a century of iron mining. The byway ends in Grand Rapids.

4

North Shore Drive
Superior National Forest

General description: A 58-mile route between the shores of Lake Superior and the rocky inland hills.

Special attractions: Lake Superior, camping, fishing, hiking, bicycling, historic sites, autumn colors, resorts, wildlife, downhill and cross-country skiing, snowmobiling.

Location: Northeast Minnesota on the Superior National Forest. The byway travels Minnesota State Highway 61 between Schroeder and the national forest boundary 11 miles southwest of Grand Portage.

Byway route number: Minnesota State Highway 61.

Travel season: Year-round.

Camping: Two state park campgrounds. Seven national forest campgrounds within 15 miles of the byway.

Services: All traveler services in Grand Marais. All services, with limited availability, in Schroeder, Tofte, and Lutsen.

Nearby attractions: Boundary Waters Wilderness Canoe Area, Grand Portage National Monument, Quetico Provincial Park in Canada.

For more information: See the appendix for contact information.

 ## The Drive

Lake Superior provides an ever-changing variety of moods to travelers on the North Shore Drive. Pounding storms alternate with peaceful sunsets and white-capped waves. To the west, rocky hillsides rise up to 1,500 feet above the lake and waterfalls pour over ledges in a rush to the lake. The two-lane road is paved and very busy—the busiest highway in Minnesota. Shoulder widths vary, but there are numerous pullouts for scenic viewing. This byway is part of the well-known Lake Superior Circle Tour, crossing three states and Canada. It is a popular resort region and you may encounter joggers and bicyclers on the route.

Weather along the North Shore is moderated by Lake Superior, which keeps the shoreline lagging behind seasonal changes inland. Spring and summer are cooler, and fall and winter are warmer than the rest of the state. In summer, daytime temperatures vary according to wind direction. When winds blow from the east, temperatures can hover in the 50s and 60s. West

Drive 4: North Shore Drive
Superior National Forest

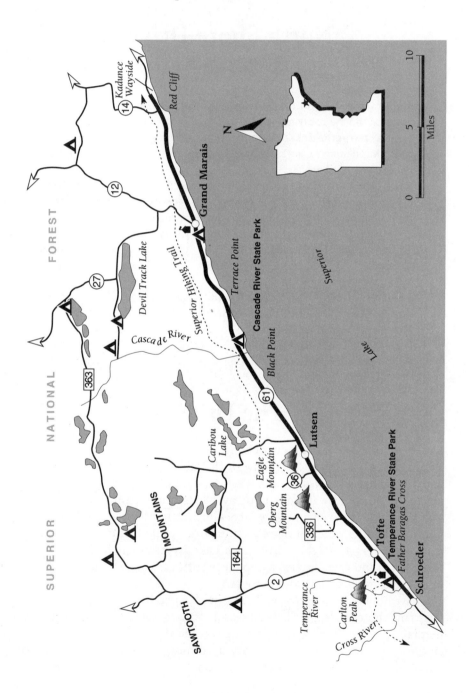

winds bring warmer temperatures up to 85 degrees. The rainiest times, generally accompanied by dense fog, are from about mid-May to early July. The driest months are August and September. Expect temperatures in the 30s and 40s along the shore in autumn, while the interior is 10 to 20 degrees colder. Winter is generally sunny, with temperatures dropping below zero and snow covering the ground from about mid-November to late March.

The byway is very scenic when driven from either direction. West to east provides bigger vistas over Lake Superior, while east to west allows more views of the big ships heading into the harbor at Duluth. The microclimate along the shore supports trees unable to withstand the cold at the top of the adjacent ridges. Red maples, sugar maples, quaking aspen, and white birch along the byway enliven autumn with their bright colors.

If traveling west to east, the byway begins at the Cross River in Schroeder. Stop to admire sheets of river water glistening down the granite faces, then walk onto the tiny peninsula to see the memorial to Father Baraga. He was sent to Duluth in 1843 to start a mission but was shipwrecked here and decided this was where he should set up the mission. Along with the memorial, weather-beaten redcedar and a few hardy black and red spruce adorn the rocky peninsula. There is a good view of rounded boulders on the rocky shoreline and bays on either side.

Temperance River State Park is bisected on the highway. Water cascades off the adjacent mountains into Lake Superior, while the deep river gorge funnels numerous waterfalls through its volcanic stone walls. Brook, brown, and rainbow trout are stocked in both the Temperance and the Cross rivers. Hikers can walk on 8 miles of trails. One trail leads to the Superior Hiking Trail, which offers more than 200 miles of maintained trail along the ridge of the Sawtooth Mountains.

Stop at the district ranger station in Tofte for national forest information and permits for the Boundary Waters Canoe Area. Tofte has interesting little arts and crafts shops. Nearby, you can take a short side trip north on Cook County Road 2 to the Carlton Park Trailhead at the top of the first big ridge. This very short, very steep trail climbs up to 1,600-foot Carlton Peak in just 0.25 mile. It's worth it. The views sweep east over Lake Superior and west into the Sawtooth Mountains. The Sawtooths rise abruptly from the lake along the scenic byways then stretch west into a broad plateau. They include the highest point in Minnesota—2,301-foot Eagle Mountain.

A good place to hike a portion of the Superior Trail is at Oberg Mountain. Drive north a few miles on Forest Road 336 then climb to the rocky bluffs at the top of the mountain. A 360-degree view is your reward.

Lutsen is one of the oldest resorts in the state. Downhill and cross-country skiing and other activities are offered.

A side trip north on Minnesota State Highway 4 leads past Caribou

The North Shore Drive travels along the shoreline of Lake Superior.
SUPERIOR NATIONAL FOREST PHOTO

Lake to the turnoffs to two national forest campgrounds. The soils at the top of the ridge are thin and rocky from repeated glaciation. The vegetation is known as a boreal forest, characterized by upland black spruce swamps and mixed stands of balsam fir, ponderosa pine, white birch, and quaking aspen. You may be lucky enough to spot a moose, black bear, or timber wolf. Easier to spot are deer, beavers, otters, eagles, osprey, peregrine falcons, loons, and ruffed grouse.

Fishing is a popular activity in the Superior National Forest. Anglers fish the small lakes for walleye, northern pike, bass, lake trout, and various panfish. The salmon run in autumn and smelt run in springtime. For competitive anglers, Lake Superior offers trophy-size fish.

The byway crests a rise and Black Point offers a sweeping view of the glistening waters of Lake Superior. On a clear day you can see the lighthouse at Grand Marais and the profile of the Sawtooth Mountains rising from the lake.

Cascade River State Park has ten streams within its boundaries. Waterfalls and gorges, deer and chipmunks add allure to the park. You can walk along the river to Cascade Falls on one of the 15 miles of hiking trails.

The byway continues east to Terrace Point, which has a nice sand beach for swimming. You may emerge blue, though—the water in Lake Superior stays about 52 degrees F year-round.

Grand Marais is a center for arts and crafts festivals and regional celebrations. The ranger station has national forest information. The harbor is a nice place to sit and watch the boats sail in and out. The municipal park allows camping and the lighthouse juts out from Circular Harbor. Visitors may want to tour St. Francis Xavier church and the Colvill Homestead. For a different perspective, drive north on Minnesota State Highway 12 to a scenic overlook of the city and harbor. Grand Marais has plenty of winter activities, from the famous John Beargrease Sled Dog Marathon to cross-country skiing and snowmobiling.

Continuing east on the byway, Red Cliff provides another view of the lake and mountains. The scenic byway ends at the national forest boundary at Kadunce Wayside Rest Area.

5

Great Divide Highway

Chequamegon National Forest

General description: A 29-mile paved highway through forests and rolling hills, past lakes, streams, and marshes.

Special attractions: Outstanding fishing in several lakes and streams, hunting, colorful foliage, historic logging-camp sites, and abundant wildlife.

Location: Northwest Wisconsin on the Chequamegon National Forest, southeast of Superior. The byway travels Wisconsin Route 77 on national forest land between Hayward and Glidden.

Byway route number: Wisconsin Route 77.

Travel season: Year-round.

Camping: There are no campgrounds located on the byway. However, there are three national forest campgrounds within a short drive, with 93 sites, water, picnic tables, fire rings, and vault toilets. No hookups.

Services: All services available in Hayward. Gas, phone, and food in Clam Lake and Glidden. Lodging at various byway resorts.

Nearby attractions: National Fresh Water Fishing Hall of Fame, Historyland, American Birkebeiner cross-country ski race, Lumberjack World Championships, Chequamegon Fat Tire Festival, Grandview Firehouse 50 Race.

For more information: See the appendix for contact information.

 The Drive

Located in the middle of the Chequamegon National Forest, the Great Divide Highway travels an obscure line that separates water flowing north to Lake Superior from water flowing south to the Gulf of Mexico. The two-lane paved road underwent extensive reconstruction in 1989. Traffic is light, allowing travelers a chance to enjoy the scenery of Wisconsin's northern lakes and timber country.

Weather conditions are variable in northern Wisconsin. Summer high temperatures are commonly around 80 with lows in the 60s, but cold fronts can drop daytime highs to the 50s. June and July are the only months in which an occasional nighttime frost is not normally expected. Winter temperatures range from daytime highs of 40 degrees to overnight lows of minus 40, though average temperatures are highs in the 20s with lows in the single digits.

Drive 5: Great Divide Highway

Chequamegon National Forest

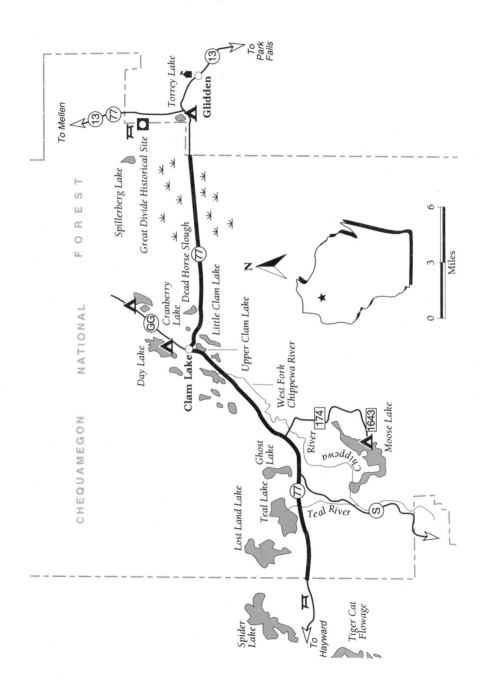

The community of Hayward is known as the home of world-record muskies because of a series of fish caught in the area during the 1940s. Set among a number of both natural and man-made flowages, it is easy to see why tourism is the number-one industry, though logging is not far behind.

The scenic byway begins at the national forest boundary near Tiger Cat Flowage. Driving east from Hayward, you will find a number of resorts and tourism-related businesses lining the road, but the natural beauty of the area becomes more prevalent the farther you get from Hayward.

The landscape along the scenic byway varies. The topography features both rolling hills and lowland areas, with American larches, spruces, pines, aspens, and maples predominating. Several noteworthy mixed forest stands are also found along the way, including white and yellow birches, hemlocks, basswoods, white ashes, and balsam firs. In autumn, the hardwoods and larches provide a spectacular display. Colors usually peak during the last week of September.

The lakes and forests of the area provide good habitat for a number of abundant wildlife species, as well as endangered species. White-tailed deer, black bears, and ruffed grouse are commonly hunted on the Chequamegon National Forest. Hunting has long been a popular fall tradition in the area, dating back to the early settlers whose winter survival depended upon the autumn hunt. In the late 1800s and early 1900s, visiting hunters traveled by railroad for days to reach this popular spot. Today the region is hunted lightly compared with other areas of the state, but it is known for producing large-bodied, trophy-racked deer. And every year, northwestern Wisconsin produces more black bears for hunters than any other region of the state. Deer are especially abundant along the roadsides just after the snow melts in spring and again during the breeding season in fall. Drive with extra caution at these times.

Good fishing lakes along the route include Round, Spider, Lost Land, Teal, Ghost, Moose, Day, Upper Clam, and Lower Clam, as well as the Tiger Cat flowage. All have public access with adequate boat-launching facilities. Muskellunge, huge fish that must be at least 32 inches long before they can legally be kept, are commonly found in these lakes. Fine-tasting walleyes inhabit all but Day Lake. Crappies also provide an exceptional fishery.

The mournful cry of the common loon is often heard on the lakes along the Great Divide Highway and bald eagles and ospreys can be seen soaring overhead. Their appearance can be the perfect cap to a good day of fishing.

Resorts are located on most of the lakes mentioned, but true wilderness fishing can be experienced on Moose and Day lakes. Both are actually flowages that provide a home to a wide variety of creatures, such as great blue herons, muskrats, beavers, and many species of ducks. It is quite common on these lakes to be fishing within only 50 yards of deer that come to

A young child examines wildflowers near the beach at Day Lake along the Great Divide Highway. STEVEN C. HEITING PHOTO

the water's edge to feed on aquatic plants. Most of the land around these lakes is national forest retained in a wild state.

At the southern end of Ghost Lake, where Ghost Creek crosses the scenic byway, is a dam left over from the logging era.

You can reach a national forest campground on Moose Lake by driving 7.5 miles south on Forest Road 174, about 10 miles west of Clam Lake. It has 15 sites, a boat launch, and a swimming area.

The last 7 miles of the byway heading toward Clam Lake generally follow the West Fork of the Chippewa River.

The Day Lake Campground is located 0.70 mile north of the byway, on Ashland County Road GG. This campground has 66 sites, a boat launch, picnic area, two swimming areas, and barrier-free access. Also on Ashland County Road GG, 3.5 miles north of the byway, is the East Twin Lake Campground, with 12 sites, a picnic area, and a boat launch.

Besides hunting, fishing, camping, swimming, boating, picnicking, and exploring, other recreational activities along this route include snowmobiling, hiking, biking, and cross-country skiing.

Clam Lake, a tiny community in southern Ashland County, once served as a hub for logging and fishing camps in the late 1800s and early 1900s. Wisconsin Route 77 evolved as a winding tote road in the 1890s, on which horse teams pulled large loads of lumbermen's supplies to the lumber camps of the Clam Lake area. Wagon and buggies traversed these tote roads during snow-free periods, while horse-drawn sleds were the only means of transportation in winter.

Glidden writer Joe A. Moran referred to the 18-mile tote road between Glidden and Clam Lake as a "seven-hour ordeal of lurching jolts through quagmire and the devil knows what, over hogbacks for a score of miles." The tote road between Clam Lake and Hayward "wiggled through untouched wilderness, where the hemlock parks were as velvet to one's tread," Moran wrote in the 1800s. Frederick Weyerhaeuser, a famous lumber baron, owned and inspected large tracts of white pine in the Clam Lake area.

A number of logging-camp sites as well as an old fire tower and Civilian Conservation Corps (CCC) camp are located along this scenic byway. The national forest has pamphlets detailing the exact locations.

Today the exuberance of a child with a first fish, the splash of a swimmer, the huffing and puffing of hikers and bicyclists, the swish of cross-country skiers, and the whine of snowmobile engines have replaced the ring of the logger's axe, but the land remains mostly wild. Scattered old-growth white pines stand as a reminder of the day when lumbering, not vacationing, was king of northern Wisconsin.

—*Steven C. Heiting*

6

Heritage Drive
Nicolet National Forest

General description: A scenic drive through a hardwood forest in a region rich in history.

Special attractions: Hiking, picnicking, boating, swimming, Blackjack Springs and Headwaters wilderness areas, historical buildings, autumn foliage.

Location: Northeast Wisconsin on the Nicolet National Forest. The byway travels two roads that form a Y—the Military Road between Wisconsin State Highway 32 and Wisconsin State Highway 70, just east of the communities of Three Lakes and Eagle River; and east from Military Road onto Butternut Road, ending at Franklin Lake Campground.

Byway route numbers: Forest Road 2178 and Forest Road 2181.

Travel season: Year-round.

Camping: Four national forest campgrounds within 2 miles of the byway, with picnic tables, fire grates, toilets, and drinking water.

Services: No traveler services available on the byway. All services in nearby Eagle River or Three Lakes.

Nearby attractions: Resorts, Eagle River Chain of Lakes, Three Lakes museum, winter sports.

For more information: See the appendix for contact information.

 The Drive

Heritage Drive consists of two connecting roads that form a Y shape. Freshwater lakes and forests of northern hardwoods and pines characterize this area. The two-lane roads are paved and mostly narrow. Traffic is moderate in the summer and fall, and light the rest of the year.

Daytime summer temperatures vary from the mid 70s to the low 90s, with occasional thunderstorms. Fall and spring daytime temperatures range from the 40s to the 70s. Winter is usually below freezing, occasionally dipping down below zero. Snow covers the ground between December and March.

The byway is scenic driven from either direction. When driven south to north, begin at the junction of Wisconsin State Highway 32 and the Military Road (Forest Road 2178). The terrain is flat or gently rolling and the

Drive 6: Heritage Drive
Nicolet National Forest

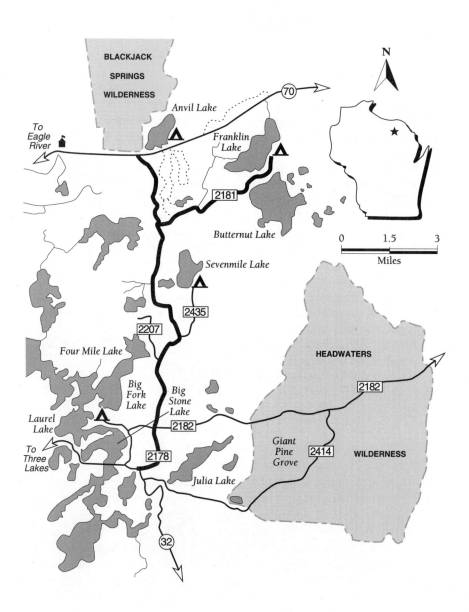

highway travels through national forest interspersed with private property. Pockets of large, old-growth white and red pines can be seen from the road, as well as northern hardwoods such as red maples, sugar maples, white birch, and yellow birch. Autumn colors are lovely.

Take a side trip east on Forest Road 2182 into Headwaters Wilderness. The 20,000 acres of wetlands and dry uplands provide opportunities to explore bogs and black spruce swamps. Orchids are one of the many wildflowers to adorn this wilderness. Beavers are abundant, as well as eastern white-tailed deer. Deer hunting is popular in autumn. An occasional timber wolf moves through the area. In spring you can see great blue herons nesting in their rookery.

The Pine River usually has enough water for canoeing, or you may wish to walk through Giant Pine Grove. To get to this mile-long, lovely hike through virgin white pines, travel east on Forest Road 2182, then southwest on Forest Road 2414. The trail is clearly marked and easy to follow.

A few miles west of the byway, Laurel Lake Campground has 12 sites in a grove of big white pines. Anglers fish for musky, walleye, bass, and northern pike, and boaters find access to the 50-mile-long Three Lakes/ Eagle River Chain of Lakes.

A tiny pond nestles in an opening in the forest along Heritage Drive.
Nicolet National Forest photo

The byway follows an ancient, well-worn Indian route originating from Green Bay on Lake Michigan and ending along Lake Superior's Keweenaw Peninsula. Native Americans used this area for at least 4,000 years prior to European settlement. Early white settlers used the trail as a mail route. In the late 1860s it was developed as a military transportation road and provided access to the rich timberlands of northern Wisconsin.

The byway meanders north through a beautiful forest. Conifers including red pine, jack pine, eastern white pine, hemlock, tamarack, cedar, spruce, and balsam fir provide a deep green contrast to the various northern hardwoods. In autumn, blazing reds, yellows, and oranges adorn sugar maples, red maples, paper birches, yellow birches, basswoods, and quaking aspens. Wildflowers along the byway include trillium, Dutchman's breeches, orchids, wild iris, and daisies.

A side trip northwest on Forest Road 2207 (Old Military Road) leads to Four Mile Lake and the Sam Campbell Memorial Trail. This 2-mile self-guided footpath encounters a wide variety of native vegetation, including a white cedar swamp, old-growth red pines, bogs, black spruce, and upland hardwoods. The trail is very pretty, with lots of gentle ups and downs along its winding course.

Continuing north on the byway, you'll see big stands of jack pines, planted in the 1930s by the Civilian Conservation Corps (CCC). Openings in this corridor of trees provide glimpses of wetlands and bogs. Turn off the byway on Forest Road 2435 to Sevenmile Lake Campground, which has 27 sites perched on a hill above the lake. There is a nice sandy swimming beach and a good hiking trail. The trail leads from the campground southeast to several small lakes, passing under big red pines and crossing a boardwalk over a cedar swamp.

Wildlife you may spot in the Nicolet National Forest includes white-tailed deer, pine martens, fishers, black bears, beavers, and raccoons. Bird watchers will delight in seeing bald eagles, osprey, great blue herons, loons, and many species of owls, hawks, and ducks. Songbirds are abundant and include warblers, vireos, wrens, thrushes, and finches.

Near its northern terminus, the byway offers two choices for travel. Turn east onto Butternut Road (Forest Road 2181), or continue north on the Military Road. A trip up Butternut Road is very pleasant, winding through stands of old, large hemlocks and northern hardwoods. The road provides access to excellent cross-country ski trails, then travels past Butternut Lake to end at Franklin Lake Campground and Picnic Area. The campground provides 77 sites, a swimming beach, and a boat launch. Summer evening ranger-led interpretive programs are sometimes offered. Topics include naturalist programs on loons, eagles, osprey, and archaeology.

A 1-mile interpretive nature trail offers an easy walk along the eskers and potholes of this glacially carved region. Old-growth white pines tower overhead and an unspoiled shoreline beckons swimmers. You can enhance the hike by following 13-mile-long Hidden Lakes Trail. Listen for the distinctive call of a loon on the lakes as you stroll by. Many other hiking trails allow you to fully explore this region.

To complete driving the scenic byway, return to the Military Road and turn north. A few miles ahead, the Anvil Lake National Recreation Trail provides 12 miles of summer hiking and winter-groomed cross-country skiing. Maps of the trail system are available at various trailheads.

The scenic byway ends at the junction of Military Road and Wisconsin State Highway 70. One mile east on Wisconsin State Highway 70, Anvil Lake Campground has 18 sites in the hardwoods. Some sites overlook the lake. The swimming beach is very popular and the 380-acre lake offers good fishing opportunities. Hikers can stretch out on a 6-mile walk to Franklin Lake Campground.

7

Black River Scenic Byway

Ottawa National Forest

General description: An 11.5-mile paved route through hardwood forests and past numerous waterfalls to a historic harbor on Lake Superior.

Special attractions: Skiing and ski jump, unique geology, waterfalls, hiking, camping, boating, mining history, Black River National Scenic River, Porcupine Mountains, old-growth hemlocks, scenic gorge, Lake Superior.

Location: The northwest corner of Michigan's upper peninsula, on the Ottawa National Forest. The byway runs from Auvinen's Corner (junction of Airport Road, County Road 204 and Black River Road, County Road 513) just north of U.S. Highway 2, to Black River Harbor.

Byway route number: County Road 513, also known as Black River Road.

Travel season: Year-round. Trails not maintained in winter.

Camping: One national forest campground with forty sites, picnic tables, flush toilets, playground, and fire rings.

Services: All services in Ironwood and Bessemer. Limited services in Black River Harbor.

Nearby attractions: Lake Superior; Big Powderhorn, Mt. Zion, Indianhead Mountain Resort, and Blackjack Mountain ski areas; Lake Gogebic State Park; Porcupine Mountains Wilderness State Park.

For more information: See the appendix for contact information.

 The Drive

The Black River Scenic Byway provides terrific recreation and scenery in just 11 miles of the northwest corner of Michigan's upper peninsula. The two-lane road is paved and has frequent turnouts. Traffic is usually light, except during August.

The weather in this region is generally dry and mild in the summers, with warmer temperatures in the 70s. Autumn and spring are fairly wet, with temperatures in the 40s and 50s. Winters temperatures range between 0 and 20, with an average annual snowfall of 195 inches.

Beginning at Auvinen's Corner, the byway heads north through a mature hardwood forest. Very large old hemlocks and Eastern white pines

Drive 7: Black River Scenic Byway
Ottawa National Forest

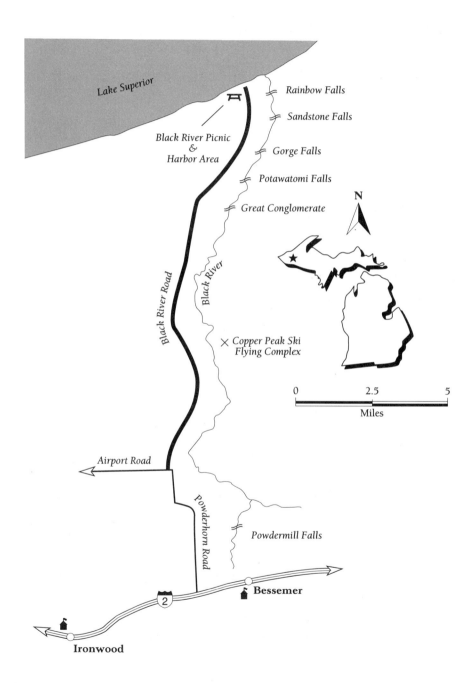

provide a magnificent ceiling to the gorge carved by the Black River, a National Scenic River. The river has cut through the soft sedimentary rock, exposing quartzite, iron, and ancient lava flows, and creating spectacular falls and rapids. The river is so named for its brownish color, the result of organic acids and naturally occurring dyes from swamps adjacent to the river's headwaters. A plant species unique to this area is the American yew, thriving due to the rich deciduous forest and less deer herbivory in this area.

Forest inhabitants include black bears, flying squirrels, red fox, white-tailed deer, ruffed grouse, and snowshoe hares. Bald eagles, barred owls, and goshawks are year-round residents and fairly easy to spot if you're alert. A rare toothwort grows on the banks of the Black River.

About 6 miles from the start of the byway, park at a designated pullout to access the North Country National Scenic Trail (not far from the Copper Peak Ski Flying Facility). This route runs 3,200 miles, from the Appalachian Trail in Vermont to the Lewis and Clark Trail in North Dakota, traversing seven states. The section along the Black River Scenic Byway parallels the river for 5 miles, providing the best viewing of the waterfalls and surrounding forest. You can hike a short piece or go the distance.

Driving north on the byway, take a gander at Copper Peak Ski Flying Complex. This ski jump, at 17 stories high, is the largest in the Northern Hemisphere. Ride an elevator or chairlift to the top for a knockout view of the Porcupine Mountains. Some say you can see three states from your vantage point. The ski jump is located on the Chippewa Mining Company's old copper mining headquarters.

There are five waterfalls with viewing decks accessible from the byway. The first is Great Conglomerate. It's a 0.75-mile hike to view this 40-foot double drop. Return to your vehicle to drive to the next falls or continue on this trail that connects with the North Country Trail, taking you downstream to some of the other falls. Make it a round-trip by hiking the river and then hiking the roadway back to your car. A round-trip from Great Conglomerate to Gorge and Potawatomi waterfalls would take roughly one and one-half hours. A round-trip from Great Conglomerate to the Black River Harbor would take between 3 and 4 hours. These trails can be fairly rugged in certain areas, with a lot of ridges, steps, and steep grades.

The beautiful Potawatomi Falls, 130 feet wide with a 30-foot drop, is accessible for people with disabilities. Rainbow Falls viewed from the east side of the river is a favorite of photographers. Anglers cast for brook trout above Rainbow Falls and try for steelhead and salmon below the falls. Because many of the streams in the area have no developed trails leading to them, anglers must be quite determined in order to get there.

The byway ends in Black River Harbor, site of a historic trout-fishing

The Black River seen from the Rainbow Falls Overlook. OTTAWA NATIONAL FOREST PHOTO

village established in the 1920s. The USDA Forest Service built the beautiful suspension bridge across the river in the late 1960s. The Civilian Conservation Corps (CCC) built a combination picnic shelter with fireplace and restrooms in the late 1930s. The recreation area includes a boat launch, campground, and 65-table picnic area. A harbor concessionaire provides limited services from Memorial Day through September. The campground has 40 paved sites, flush toilets, dumping station, fire rings, and water. Boating and fishing are the major summer activities. The harbor is a popular access to Lake Superior. The Porcupines provide a scenic backdrop as you stroll the shores of Lake Superior.

8

Whitefish Bay Scenic Byway

Hiawatha National Forest

General description: A 27-mile road along Lake Superior's Whitefish Bay, past beaches and through northern hardwood forests.

Special attractions: Clean sand beaches, historic lighthouse and museum, campgrounds, boat launches, national fish hatchery.

Location: Eastern Upper Peninsula of Michigan on the Hiawatha National Forest, west of Sault Ste. Marie. The byway travels Curly Lewis Highway (Forest Road 3150) and Forest Road 42 west from Brimley to the junction of Forest Road 42 and Michigan Route 123 .

Byway route numbers: Forest Road 3150 and Forest Road 42.

Travel season: Year-round.

Camping: Two national forest campgrounds with fire rings, picnic tables, drinking water, and toilets. Campgrounds open mid-May through mid-October.

Services: Gas, groceries, and restaurant in Bay Mills. All services in nearby Brimley, Sault Ste. Marie, Paradise, and Newberry.

Nearby attractions: Soo Locks, Tahquamenon Falls State Park, Brimley State Park, Great Lakes Shipwreck Museum, North Country hiking trail.

For more information: See the appendix for contact information.

 The Drive

Whitefish Bay Scenic Byway travels the shoreline of Whitefish Bay through white birches, pines, and spruce. The two-lane paved highway has frequent scenic turnouts, as well as one-lane dirt side roads that lead through the forest.

Summer temperatures range from the 50s to an idyllic 80 degrees. Although Lake Superior summer temperatures seldom rise above 68 degrees, the shallow bays are swimmable, if invigorating. Winter brings snowfalls averaging 100 inches a year and temperatures can dip below zero. Cloudiness and precipitation are fairly constant and heavy fogs reach a peak between August and October.

St. Mary's River at Sault Ste. Marie brought early explorers, missionaries, and fur traders through the area, followed by timbermen who felled the virgin white pine forests and opened the area for further development. Except

Drive 8: Whitefish Bay Scenic Byway

Hiawatha National Forest

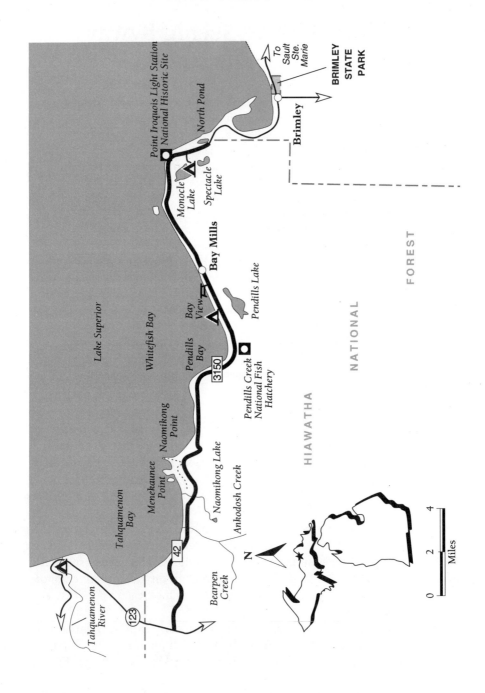

for scattered summer cottages, the area shows little disturbance. Forests are second-growth and the lakes are unspoiled by development. Tourism and small industry form the basis of the area's economy, with Lake Superior the main attraction. Superior can be temperamental. Its glassy surface can suddenly be rent by crashing waves brought in by gale-force winds.

Driving west from Sault Ste. Marie and Brimley, the scenic byway begins at the national forest boundary in a hardwood forest with scattered white pines and jack pines. The predominant hardwood species are birch, maple, and oak, which blaze red, orange, and gold during late September and early October.

Monocle Lake is near the byway's eastern entrance. There is serenity and silence in this forest campground, interrupted only by the sound of birds. Take the short drive to the Mission Hill Overlook for a panoramic view of the area and enjoy the swimming beach. The campground has 39 sites.

A few miles west on the byway is the Point Iroquois Light Station. The light was activated in 1858 and the existing two-story brick keeper's residence and the light tower were built in 1870. An automated beacon replaced the light in 1962. The lighthouse museum and gift shop is open daily from May 15 through October 15 from 9 A.M. to 5 P.M. The tower is open until sunset. A footpath leads down the low bluff to the Lake Superior shoreline.

Across the wide expanse of water is the Canadian shore. Nineteen miles of accessible sand beach on the gently curving bay follow a shoreline of ancient sand dunes and glacial moraines. The bay is located on the north rim of the Michigan Basin, which was covered by glacial outwash. Scattered outcroppings of limestone and sandstone protrude from the surface. Past levels of the Great Lakes during the latest period of glaciation left generous lake-basin sand deposits.

The byway runs primarily within 0.25-mile of the shoreline and is never more than a few miles away. Whitefish Bay itself holds a double legacy: It was memorialized in Henry Wadsworth Longfellow's "Song of Hiawatha," and it is the historical site of many shipwrecks between the mid-1800s and the early 1900s. The *Edmund Fitzgerald* met her fate off Whitefish Point 20 miles to the north, an event that was the subject of a ballad by Canadian singer Gordon Lightfoot.

Forest and wildflowers line the byway, and colors change with the seasons. White trilliums introduce spring, a wild profusion of colors announces summer, and deep blue asters and chickories rival the autumn leaves. In winter, the deep-green conifers stand out against the white snow.

At Bay Mills, a small general store has groceries, ice, and gasoline.

Big Pine Picnic Area stands in a red pine forest with scatterings of

Families enjoy the wide beaches and vast views of Lake Superior and Whitefish Bay.
DIXIE FRANKLIN PHOTO

birches and maples. Bay View Campground is 1 mile farther west. The campground has 24 sites and the long sand beach is lovely. Even if the lake is too cold for swimming, the shallows stretch some distance from shore and are good for wading.

Pendill's National Fish Hatchery is an interesting stop and tours of lake-trout hatching ponds are available. There is good trout fishing in Pendill's Creek.

The trees are taller as you head west from Pendill's and they stand farther back from the roadway. Wildflowers line the route. Scenic turnouts provide views of the bay, which stretches out wide and blue on a clear day. The byway climbs up and away from the lake and then returns to the shore and its open vistas.

The North Country National Scenic Trail intersects the byway about 1 mile east of Naomikong Creek and parallels the shore through old-growth hardwoods for about 4 miles. Several turnoffs and parking areas provide access to the trail along Tahquamenon Bay.

Scenic turnouts and beachside parking areas are at the end of the byway near Michigan Route 123, giving you plenty of opportunities to enjoy the blue waters, wide skies, and sand beaches.

—*Dixie Franklin*

9

River Road

Huron-Manistee National Forest

General description: A 22-mile road alongside the scenic Au Sable River.
Special attractions: Lumberman's Monument, largo Springs Interpretive Site, paddle-wheel riverboat rides, historic and scenic sites, canoeing, trout and salmon fishing, colorful autumn foliage, beaches, camping.
Location: Northeast Michigan on the Huron National Forest, south of Alpena. The byway begins at the national forest boundary just west of Oscoda, travels the River Road west to its junction with Michigan Route 65, and continues west on Michigan Route 65 to the national forest boundary near Rollway Road.
Byway route numbers: River Road and Michigan Route 65.
Travel season: Year-round.
Camping: Two national forest campgrounds with picnic tables, fire grates, drinking water, and toilets. Campgrounds open from May 25 to October 15. One township campground with 500 sites, drinking water, and showers. Two hundred sites have hookups. Open April 1 to December 1.
Services: All services in Oscoda and in nearby Hale.
Nearby attractions: Michigan Shore-to-Shore Hiking and Riding Trail; Huron Snowmobile and ATV Trail; Eagle Run, Highbanks, and Corsair cross-country ski and hiking trails; Kiwanis Monument.
For more information: See the appendix for contact information.

 ## The Drive

River Road follows the south bank of the Au Sable River near Lake Huron. The scenic byway begins a short distance from the river's mouth at Oscoda and follows the river across low, sandy plains. The two-lane paved highway has frequent turnouts for scenic and recreational access.

Summer visitors enjoy contrasts in weather, varying from early spring and late autumn temperatures in the 50s to occasional sultry summer days of 90 degrees. Winters normally average around the 20s, with a few days below zero.

River Road follows the old Saginaw to the Mackinaw Indian Trail of the Chippewas and other Michigan tribes who inhabited the area. The byway travels through a serene landscape along the lazy river, which snakes

Drive 9: River Road

Huron-Manistee National Forest

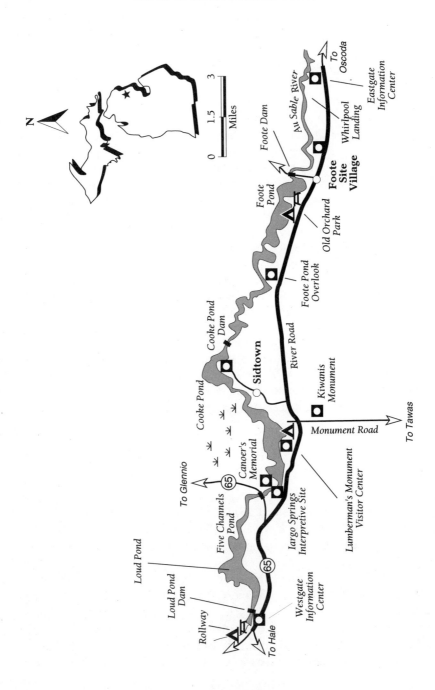

between white sandy bluffs and long corridors of green forest spires. This is a glaciated landscape of the Michigan sedimentary basin. Outwash and deltas were carved by the latest ice age.

Oscoda, on the Lake Huron shoreline, is a former lumber-mill town that now depends largely upon tourism for its livelihood. Evidence of the old logging days is visible at the concrete Au Sable Bridge, where decaying piers and log-boom sorting ponds are still visible.

Oscoda was leveled by fire in 1911 and scars of more recent blazes can be seen along River Road. Green sprouts of new vegetation in the burned areas are the result of work done by nature and the USDA Forest Service.

West on the byway, the burned area gives way to lowland timber such as maples, oaks, and ashes in the lower sites. Oaks, and red, white, and jack pines are the primary species on the upper sandy plains. The burned area, about 2,500 acres adjacent to the byway, is classified as essential habitat for the Kirtland's warbler.

A short distance west of the national forest boundary, Eastgate Information Center provides easy access to the Eagle Run cross-country ski and nature trails. Trails lead through the forest to the scenic Whirlpool canoe and boat launch. The popular Whirlpool launch is also accessible by a 0.5-mile unpaved road. This section of stream is fed by the spill from Foote Dam hydroelectric site upstream and the water is very cold.

You can fish Whirlpool from its sandy banks or from its accessible fishing pier. The Au Sable River offers anglers the chance to catch trophy-size steelhead, in addition to coho, chinook, and Atlantic salmon. Other wildlife along the byway includes white-tailed deer, wild turkeys, foxes, coyotes, and small mammals such as squirrels.

The Au Sable is slowed by a number of hydroelectric dams, forming wide, blue pools known for producing walleyes, muskellunge, bass, northern pikes, bluegills, and sunfish. Anglers, canoeists, a river paddle-wheeler, and careful boaters use the waterway, conscious of deadheads (jammed logs) left over from logging days.

Groceries and supplies are available at Foote Site Village, at the intersection of the byway and Rea Road. A short side trip on Rea Road leads to Foote Dam power site, where there are public launch ramps and a 500-foot fishing pier.

About 8 miles farther west on the byway, you can see a wide stretch of beach along Foote Pond. The colorful red, white, and blue Au Sable River Queen paddle wheeler takes passengers for cruises up and down the 1,800-acre pond, among the scattered islands, and around the forested shoreline.

Nearby, Old Orchard Park offers a campground, picnic area, playground equipment, toilets, a boat-launch area, and swimming beaches. Paved roads wind through the forested park along the banks of Foote Pond.

The scenic Au Sable River, which runs alongside River Road, provides opportunities for canoeing, riding paddle wheelers, fishing, swimming, camping, and hiking.
DIXIE FRANKLIN PHOTO

The next few miles of scenic byway cut through 50- to 60-year-old mixed red pine and jack pine forest. A short side trip on Cooke Dam Road drops down to the river through Sidtown, a small village and country store with camping and vacation supplies. The road passes beneath trees that turn spectacular colors in autumn. Several scenic turnouts provide views of Cooke Pond and fishing is good. There are boat launches above and below the dam.

A main attraction on the byway is Lumberman's Monument. The statue portrays three loggers standing over a fallen log; one has a cross-cut saw balanced over his shoulder, another wields a peavey, and the third contemplates his compass. The rustic visitors center has barrier-free access to outdoor exhibits and a 263-step wooden stairway down to Cooke Pond. Across the road, Kiwanis Monument is another historic site.

River Road continues through red and Norway pines to the Canoer's Memorial. Canoer's Memorial, erected in the early 1950s, pays tribute to the many thousands of marathon canoeists who have participated annually in a grueling 240-mile race down the Au Sable, from its headwaters near Grayling to Oscoda.

Eye-catching wildflowers along the byway include smooth asters, goldenrod, bracken ferns, blazing stars, fireweeds, and blue vervains.

Largo Springs is farther west, with 1,200 feet of boardwalk for meandering through the natural springs area. Watch for waterfowl on the quiet waters of Cooke Pond. Largo Springs also serves as the trailhead for the popular Highbanks Trail, which winds along the high bluffs of Cooke Pond and offers many panoramic views.

River Road intersects Michigan Route 65 and the scenic byway continues west. A short side trip north on Michigan Route 65 takes you across the iron Five Channel Bridge.

Rollway Campground and Picnic Area mark the western end of the scenic byway and provide access to Loud Pond.

—Dixie Franklin

10

Ohio River Scenic Byway

Hoosier National Forest

General description: A 67-mile paved route that generally follows the Ohio River though rural and wooded hilly countryside.

Special attractions: Scenic overlooks of the Ohio River, rock outcrops, historic buildings, scenic railroad, fishing, boating, camping.

Location: Southern Indiana on the Hoosier National Forest. The route runs between Corydon and Tell City.

Byway route numbers: Indiana State Highway 62, Crawford County Road 36, Perry County Road 27, and Indiana State Highway 66.

Travel season: Year-round.

Camping: Two national forest campgrounds, with 26 sites, picnic tables, fire rings or grills, vault toilets, no hookups. One state forest campground with swimming, picnicking, hiking, horse trails.

Services: All services in Corydon and Tell City. Limited services in Cannelton, Derby, Leavenworth.

Nearby attractions: Harrison-Crawford State Forest, Wyandotte Woods State Recreation Area and Caves, Ohio River Scenic Route (state and federal), Holiday World theme park, Lincoln Boyhood National Memorial, Patoka Lake, Louisville (Kentucky) and Evansville (Indiana) city attractions.

For more information: See the appendix for contact information.

 The Drive

The Ohio River Scenic Byway traverses hilly, forested terrain along the Ohio River during its journey across southern Indiana, offering outstanding vistas of the surrounding landscape of Indiana and Kentucky. Historic barns and churches, grazing livestock, and picturesque communities accent the route. The two-lane winding road is paved, and travelers move between 25 and 55 miles per hour. Occasional one-lane bridges add to the feeling of quiet travel from a bygone era. Traffic is usually light.

Summers are hot and humid, ranging from a high in the 80s and 90s with a low in the 70s. Winter temperatures run in the 30s to 50s, with minimal snowfall and some rain. Fall and spring are usually 40 to 60 during the day, dropping to the 40s during the evenings.

Drive 10: Ohio River Scenic Byway

Hoosier National Forest

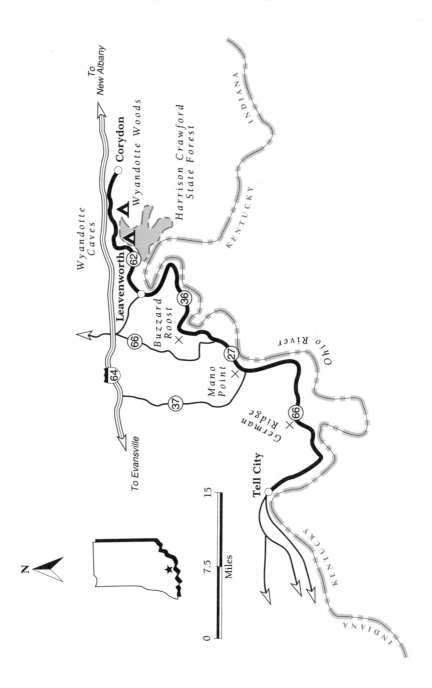

The byway is scenic traveling from either direction. When beginning in Corydon, the first capital of Indiana, take a walking tour to view its numerous historic buildings and interesting shops. Take a walk through the first capitol, built of Indiana limestone in 1816. The 1883 vintage scenic railroad is interesting, as are the numerous antique shops. Numerous other attractions are in a fairly small area, including Governor Hendricks' home, the Constitution elm, Battle of Corydon Civil War site, and the first state treasury building.

Traveling west about 7 miles, you enter the Harrison-Crawford State Forest, which contains the Wyandotte Woods State Recreation Area. Extensive recreation opportunities include 281 modern campsites. Harrison-Crawford has 25 sites with hookups, water, and showers. It also offers primitive and group camping, a 120-unit horseback rider's campground, public swimming pool, hiking trails, and a nature center. Boaters can launch on the Ohio River at Leavenworth's and Rome's public boat ramps. Canoeists generally head for the Blue River.

Drive toward Buzzard Roost, taking time to pull off and savor some exceptional views. You can see wide panoramas of Kentucky, with the oxbow of the Ohio River very evident.

Buzzard Roost Recreation Area has six sites and a pretty overlook of the Ohio River. There are benches along the trail that lead to the river bluff overlooking the river.

Mano Point provides one of the few public access points to the Ohio River along the byway. The boat ramp has a 50-boat capacity.

German Ridge Recreation Area is just north of the byway and has 20 sites and accommodates horses. The interesting rock formations are best viewed from a short 1-mile-loop hiking trail at the picnic area. Cool off at the swimming beach, or drop in a fishing line for blue gill, bass, and catfish. Rare blackjack pine and post oak grow in the rare barrens (savanna-type glades). A 22-mile multipurpose trail from German Ridge Recreation Area passes through these interesting areas.

Oaks, hickories, beeches, and maples cap the ridges. The lower valleys host ashes, tulip poplars, and sycamores. Springtime is lovely with flowering dogwoods and redbuds, but the autumn colors along the byway will knock your socks off! Summer wildflowers include trilliums, fire pinks, Indian paintbrush, buttercups, and spring beauties.

Farms are interspersed with woods on this hilly, curvy narrow road. The Ohio River is rarely lonesome, since pleasure boats, tugboats, and barges navigate the waters constantly. In places, the sheer rock cliffs plunge 400 feet to the river, providing dramatic vistas. Anglers fish for bass, catfish, sauger, crappie, carp, and sunfish.

The Ohio River meanders through the Hoosier National Forest. DAVE KISSEL PHOTO

Watchable Wildlife sites are Buzzard Roost and Little Blue River. Eastern wild turkeys and white-tailed deer abound. There are also squirrels, grouse, quail, rabbits, and great blue herons. Buzzards and hawks circle, and the many songbirds you might hear include bluebirds, robins, jays, mockingbirds, and meadowlarks.

For an instructive picnic or rest stop, stop next to Cannelton Locks and Dam to watch the barges go through the locks around the dam. Cannelton's historic district includes buildings such as St. Luke's Episcopal Church, built in 1845, and the Indiana Cotton Mill, built in 1849.

The Ohio River National Forest Scenic Byway continues on through pastoral farmland and private developments. It ends in Tell City, named for William Tell, a modern community known today for furniture making and pretzels.

The much longer state- and federally designated Ohio River Scenic Route continues through Evansville into Illinois. On the eastern edge of Indiana, the byway passes through Ohio.

11

Shawnee Hills on the Ohio Scenic Byway

Shawnee National Forest

General description: A 70-mile route through the historic and scenic features of the Shawnee Hills and the Ohio River.

Special attractions: Cave-In-Rock, Trail of Tears National Historic Trail, Garden of the Gods, hiking, Tower Rock, historic buildings, locks and dam.

Location: Southeastern Illinois on the Shawnee National Forest. The byway travels between Smithland Locks and Dams on the south and Mitchellsville on the north.

Byway route numbers: Illinois State Highway 34 between Mitchellsville and a few miles south of Herod; Karbers Ridge Road (Gallatin County Road 13 and Hardin County Road 9) along Karbers Ridge between Illinois State Highway 34 and Illinois State Highway 1; Illinois State Highway 1 from the junction of Karbers Ridge Road to Cave-In-Rock; Illinois State Highway 146 between Illinois State Highway 1 near Cave-In-Rock and Golconda; Pope County Road 1 between Golconda and Smithland Locks and Dam.

Travel season: Year-round.

Camping: Six national forest campgrounds on or near the byway, with picnic tables, fire grates, toilets, and drinking water.

Services: Traveler services in Cave-In-Rock, Elizabethtown, Rosiclare, and Golconda, with limited availability.

Nearby attractions: Lake Glendale Recreation Area, Dixon Springs State Park, Glen O. Jones Lake, The Old Slave House, Lake of Egypt Recreation Area.

For more information: See the appendix for contact information.

 The Drive

Shawnee Hills on the Ohio Scenic Byway tours through hills and ridgetops before dropping down to follow the Ohio River. The road is two-lane and paved, with occasional turnouts. Traffic is generally heavy and moves at 40 to 55 miles per hour. Karbers Ridge is especially busy in spring and fall. South of Golconda tends to receive moderate use.

Drive 11: Shawnee Hills on the Ohio Scenic Byway

Shawnee National Forest

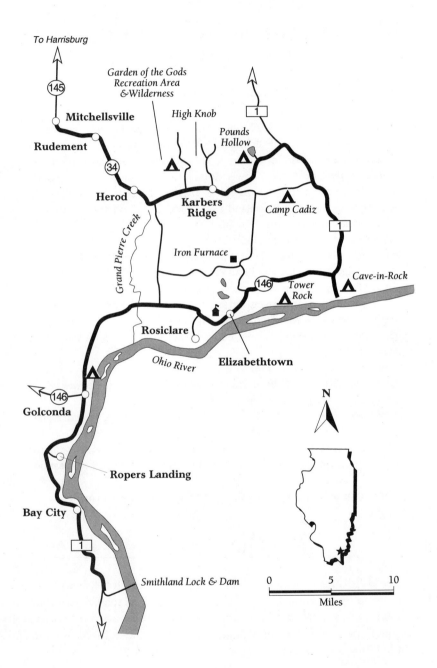

Summer temperatures range from 70 to 90, with high humidity. Spring and fall are between 65 and 80, with less humidity and frequent rain. Winter temperatures average in the 30s and 40s, and snow generally melts fairly quickly.

The byway is diverse and scenic driven in either direction. Beginning in Mitchellsville (about 6 miles south of Harrisburg), you'll drive through open pasturelands and get a preview of the forested Shawnee Hills ahead. The byway follows Illinois State Highway 34 southeast, and enters the Shawnee National Forest. The route rolls up and down the hills, climbing through pretty pastoral scenes and woodlands.

The byway turns east and climbs up Karbers Ridge. The forest is composed of oaks and hickories, along with tulip poplars, elms, maples, cedars, dogwoods, redbuds, sumacs, and sassafras. Spring-flowering shrubs and autumn leaves are absolutely breathtaking.

Take a side trip north to Garden of the Gods, an area of fascinating sandstone rock formation. There is picnicking, the campground has 12 sites, and interconnecting footpaths and horse trails allow you to explore easily. A quarter-mile long barrier-free path (completed in 1992) leads to a view point above the cliffs, where you'll see the Shawnee Hills and Garden of the Gods Wilderness. Look for unique rocks such as Anvil, Mushroom, and Camel.

The sandstone outcrops and bluffs visible at Garden of the Gods were deposited as sand and mud in a 300-million-year-old marine and river environment. Wind, annual freeze/thaw cycles, and melting glaciers eroded the soft rock into valleys and the weird shapes we see today. Oxidizing iron causes the reddish streaks and bands you see on exposed rocks.

Back on the byway, the route traverses Karbers Ridge. A side trip north to High Knob provides extensive views of the Shawnee National Forest, including the east side of Garden of the Gods.

The national forest shelters a wide variety of wildlife: 237 species of resident or migrating birds; 79 species of amphibians and reptiles; 48 species of mammals; and 109 species of fish.

Continue east on the byway then take another side trip north. Pounds Hollow Recreation Area provides opportunities to picnic, hike, camp, swim, boat, and fish. The campground has 76 sites, a play area, and drinking water. Boats can be rented, and anglers fish for largemouth bass, channel catfish, and sunfish. Campfire interpretive programs are presented on holiday weekends in the summer.

The Rim Rock National Recreation Trail wanders less than 1 mile through hardwoods and cedar, goes near the Ox-Lot Cave and through Fat Man Squeeze, encircles the Rim Rock Escarpment, and provides a pretty view of Pounds Hollow Lake. You can continue on to the Beaver Trail and walk around the lake.

Camel Rock juts out among the rock outcrops in Garden of the Gods, along the Shawnee Hills on the Ohio Scenic Byway. SHAWNEE NATIONAL FOREST PHOTO

Back on the byway, travel east to Illinois State Highway 1, then turn south. Another side trip leads about 3 miles west to Camp Cadiz, which has 11 sites, drinking water, a horse corral, and remnants of the old Civilian Conservation Corps (CCC) camp structures. This is the eastern trailhead for the River-to-River Trail, popular with horseback riders and backpackers.

Cave-In-Rock State Park lies at the southern end of Illinois State Highway 1, right on the Ohio River. A high limestone bluff faces the river, and a 55-foot-wide entrance arch leads into Cave-In-Rock, which extends about 160 feet back into the cliff. The cave sheltered numerous river bandits and other unsavory characters in the 1800s. Today you can look down into the cave from above. The cave was used in filming the movie "How the West Was Won."

The park also offers boating, fishing, hiking, camping, picnicking, and a resort facility. The restaurant features fresh Ohio River catfish dinners.

The byway goes back north on Illinois State Highway 1 a few miles, then turns west on Illinois State Highway 146. Tower Rock is the highest point on the Ohio River. The campground has 35 sites in the sycamores and cottonwoods along the banks of the Ohio. A quarter-mile trail goes near the top of Tower Rock and provides a splendid view of the river and islands and the surrounding hills of Illinois and Kentucky. A boat ramp provides access to the Ohio River.

Elizabethtown has several historic structures, such as the Rose Hotel, the First Baptist Church, and the Hardin County Courthouse. A ranger station has national forest information, maps, and permits. Take a side trip north to Iron Furnace Recreation Area. Interpretive signs explain the workings of this furnace, which produced pig iron in the 1900s. The furnace was rebuilt to its present form in 1967. A pleasant 0.5-mile interpretive trail follows Big Creek and points out natural and historic features.

Canoeists can enjoy floating Big Grand Pierre Creek. A popular float begins on Illinois State Highway 146 and goes about 4 miles to the Ohio River then continues on down the river to Golconda.

Rosiclare hosts the oldest mining company in the United States, mining for lead and fluorspar. The byway continues through low rolling hills, cultivated fields, pasturelands, and small settlements. The forested Shawnee Hills lie to the north.

Many of Golconda's buildings are listed on the National Register of Historic Places. Visit the museum and pick up a guide for the walking tour, which meanders through "silk stocking row" and the estates on the bluff. Nearby, the new marina caters to boaters and anglers. Fishing for bass, bluegill, crappie, and catfish is excellent.

The Cherokee Indian Trail of Tears passes through this area. In 1938, 15,000 Cherokees were forced to leave their homes, and were marched nearly 1,000 miles away. At least 4,000 Cherokee died along the way, from malnutrition, cholera, and exposure. Monuments along their route mark this shameful event in our nation's history.

The byway continues south, now on County Road 1. Boat launches are provided at Roper's Landing and Bay City. The byway ends at Smithland Lock and Dam. You can watch the boats pass through the locks and tour the visitor center to learn about this interesting process.

12

Sugar Camp Scenic Byway

Mark Twain National Forest

General description: An 8.1-mile Forest Service gravel route, primarily along a ridgetop with several scenic outlooks.

Special attractions: Spring wildflowers, fall foliage, hiking, picnicking, hunting.

Location: Southwest Missouri on the Mark Twain National Forest. The byway begins 4 miles south of Roaring River State Park off of Missouri Highway 112 and follows Forest Road 197 to its junction with Missouri Highway 86 south of Eagle Rock.

Byway route number: Forest Road 197.

Travel season: Year-round.

Camping: No designated national forest campgrounds but camping is permitted along the route. One picnic area has a fireplace and grill. No toilet or water. Five campgrounds within 10 miles.

Services: All services in Cassville. Limited services in Seligman, Oakhill, Eagle Rock.

Nearby attractions: Roaring River State Park, Piney Creek Wilderness, Table Rock Lake, Eureka Springs, AK.

For more information: See the appendix for contact information.

 The Drive

The Sugar Camp Scenic Byway traverses a forested ridgetop in the southwest corner of Missouri. The two-lane road is a graded and maintained gravel route that has several turnouts for scenic viewing or hiking. Traffic is light during the week and moderate on weekends.

This area enjoys four distinct seasons. Summers can be very hot with temperatures reaching well into the 90s, with significant humidity. Autumn and spring temperatures range from the 50s to the 70s. While winters can be cold and icy or fairly mild, depending on the year.

The byway is beautiful driven from either direction. Beginning on the west end (south of Roaring River State Park), the byway starts heading east along the ridgetop. You'll notice quite a bit of relief on both sides of the road, with rugged valleys and knobs. The term "knobs" refers to the conical hills that rise above the drainages and ridges and came from the Ozark's

Drive 12: Sugar Camp Scenic Byway

Mark Twain National Forest

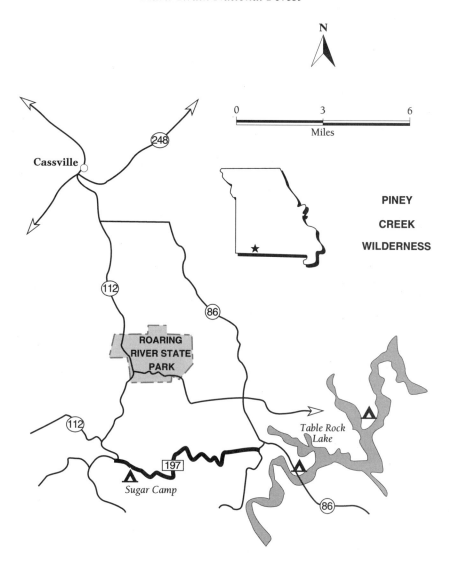

original settlers, the Scots-Irish who migrated from the Tennessee/Kentucky area.

One of the area's biggest attractions is the rainbow trout fishing at the Roaring River State Park where there are a variety of campgrounds, cabins, and the fish hatchery. Horseback riders use a variety of trails off the area, and water-skiing and other water sports are very popular at Table Rock Lake to the east. While there are no interpretive trails and ranger programs on the

A view from the Sugar Camp Scenic Byway. MARK TWAIN NATIONAL FOREST PHOTO

byway, the nearby Piney Creek Wilderness to the northeast does offer them. Pick up information on the byway's trails at the nearby Cassville Ranger Station.

About 2 miles in from the western approach, you'll come upon the Sugar Camp Look Out, with a small picnic area. Climb to the top for a great view of most of the Cassville Ranger District's rugged terrain, as well as views of Table Rock Lake.

A lot of oak and hickory trees grow in the byway's region. The area is also heavily populated with sugar maples. Settlers would camp upon the ridge for several weeks during the early spring to tap the hard maple trees for syrup. Hence the name Sugar Camp. Aside from its practical usage, the maples bring a unique color to the area's fall spectrum.

Hunters seek out the wild turkeys, squirrels, and deer of the forest while bird watchers look out for the bald eagles that visit Table Rock for its warm water fish in the winter. The other stop on the byway is the Onyx Cave Picnic Area where there are three table and fire grates. For you spelunkers, the cave is just down the hill from the picnic area.

As you continue to head east you'll find more pullouts, all affording fantastic Ozark vistas. The southeastern view from the byway gives you a good look at the White River Drainage area, which was dammed to create the lake. Table Lake has multiple campgrounds, boat launches, and resorts.

13

Glade Top Trail

Mark Twain National Forest

General description: A 23-mile, well-maintained gravel road through the glades and forests of the Ozark Plateau.

Special attractions: Wildlife, bird watching, hunting, hiking, spring blossoms, colorful autumn foliage, horseback riding.

Location: Southwest Missouri on the Mark Twain National Forest, southeast of Springfield. The byway is shaped like an upside-down Y. It begins at the national forest boundary on Forest Road 147 and travels south to Longrun, and it also travels on Forest Road 149 from the junction of Forest Road 149 and Forest Road 147 to the junction with Missouri Route 125.

Byway route numbers: Forest Road 147 and Forest Road 149.

Travel season: Year-round. Winter driving conditions may be hazardous.

Camping: No national forest campgrounds on the byway. Primitive camping permitted along the byway, except at picnic areas. Other public campgrounds are located nearby.

Services: All services in Ava. Gas and store in Thornfield. Store, phone, and gas in Bradleyville.

Nearby attractions: Hercules Glade Wilderness, Laura Ingalls Wilder home in Mansfield, old grist mills, fox-trotting horse shows in Ava, Our Lady of Assumption Abbey.

For more information: See the appendix for contact information.

 The Drive

Situated in the rolling hills of the Ozark Plateau, Glade Top Trail has changed very little since the Civilian Conservation Corps (CCC) built the two-lane gravel road in the late 1930s. The entire road is well-marked and has frequent pullouts.

Summer visitors can expect very humid weather and an average temperature of 89 degrees. Fall and spring are more moderate, and average temperatures are in the 40s through 60s. Winter ranges from 10 to 50 degrees, with precipitation falling in the form of snow or sleet. Roads may be icy in the winter.

Drive 13: Glade Top Trail
Mark Twain National Forest

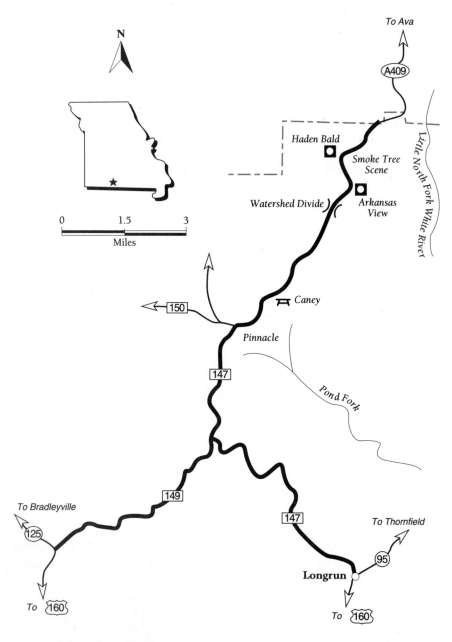

The glades are home to numerous species of wildflowers, such as purple coneflowers, columbines, Indian paintbrushes, chickories, jonquils, and daffodils. Dogwoods, redbuds, and serviceberries add to the profusion of spring color, and local communities celebrate the season with festivals and tours.

Driving the byway from north to south, the first point of interest about 1 mile from the beginning of the byway is Haden Bald, across from Smoke Tree Scene. This area is called "bald" because of the extensive, open limestone glades. Haden Bald is a State Natural Area of 40 acres. Management includes a controlled burn every four to six years, and no grazing. Other areas of the national forest permit open grazing, so watch for cattle along the road.

Bare knobs such as this were common meeting places for the Baldknobbers, bands of vigilantes who emerged primarily in Taney, Christian, and Douglas counties during a period of relative lawlessness following the Civil War. The men eventually ran amok, donning horned, white masks and conducting raids on townsfolk for several decades following the war.

Smoke Tree Scene is an interpretive site. Smoke Trees are known locally as yellowwood because of the tree's color when the bark is removed. The trees dot the entire hollow and turn magnificent deep hues of red and orange in autumn.

The flora and fauna along this trail truly accentuate the beauty of the Ozark Plateau. Limestone glades and gentle rolling hills are home to central hardwood forests of oaks, hickories, walnuts, and ashes. Redcedars, smoke trees, rare ash, junipers, and flowering trees provide more variety. Native prairie grasses line the roadway and dot the open hillsides. These grasses include big and little bluestems, and Indian grasses. Wildlife such as white-tailed deer, wild turkeys, bobwhites, squirrels, cottontail rabbits, and chipmunks inhabit the area, as do the less common roadrunners, collared lizards, pygmy rattlesnakes, scorpions, and endangered Bachman sparrows.

Arkansas View, 1.5 miles past Smoke Tree Scene, overlooks a panorama that includes the Boston Mountains, about 40 miles south. There is a picnic table and plenty of shade for an enjoyable family outing.

One mile south, Watershed Divide separates the Beaver Creek watershed to the west and the Little North Fork White River watershed to the east. This is a good place to see native hardwoods such as oaks—black, white, post, chinquapin, and northern red. Winged elm trees are also fairly common. From the divide, you can see Caney Lookout Tower to the south. The Civilian Conservation Corps (CCC) built this historic tower in 1937.

Caney Picnic Area is a very popular spot. There are picnic tables, a stationary grill, an open-air stage, restrooms, and split-rail benches. The annual Glade Top Trail Festival (or Flaming Fall Revue) is held in mid-October. This three-day event celebrates the brilliant red and orange foliage of the smoke trees and the overall beauty of the Ozarks. There are activities in Ava, such as arts and crafts shows, and a Sunday afternoon barbeque and music festival at the Caney Picnic Area.

The Glade Top Trail offers pretty views over the rolling Ozark Plateau, which is especially colorful in autumn. JOHN LOWELL LUMB PHOTO

North of the Caney parking lot, a vague trail wanders off to an interesting cave. One mile south of the picnic area is the Pinnacle, and on top of the Pinnacle is Mrs. Murray's Gold Mine. According to legend, Mrs. Murray had a vision in which she was instructed to dig on the Pinnacle to find gold. Although she never found it, evidence of her digging remains.

Local residents used to gather on the Pinnacle for church services the first Sunday in May. It was not uncommon for a crowd of 500 to be present for the all-day event.

The first white men in this area were hunters, trappers, and farmers. During the Depression years, settlers came from all areas, lured by the cheap land. The Ozarks became a melting pot for immigrants. The Lee Houseplace was a schoolhouse attended by about 40 children in the 1930s.

Eastern redcedar trees, actually members of the juniper family, are able to grow in the shallow soils atop the limestone ridges. Their distinctive, twisted shapes are easily recognized. The waxy, blue berries on the female tree are a favorite food of birds in the area, and they are also used in distilling gin.

The byway forks a few miles south of the Pinnacle. You may follow either Forest Road 147 or Forest Road 149. Forest Road 147 goes southeast and ends at Longrun, while Forest Road 149 goes southwest and ends at the junction of Forest Road 149 and Missouri Route 125. From both, you will have lovely panoramic views of farms, hills, and forest.

—John Lowell Lumb

14

Blue Buck Knob Scenic Byway

Mark Twain National Forest

General description: A 24-mile paved route through the Ozark hill country.

Special attractions: Noblett Lake Recreation Area, scenic overlooks, Ridge Runner National Recreation Trail, Blue Buck Fire Lookout, Carman Springs Wildlife Refuge.

Location: Southwest Missouri on the Mark Twain National Forest.

Byway route numbers: Missouri Route 181, Missouri Route 76, and Missouri Route AP.

Travel season: Year-round.

Camping: One national forest campground with picnic tables, vault toilets, fire rings, and no drinking water.

Services: All services in West Plains, Willow Springs, Cabool, and Mountain Grove. Limited services in Siloam Springs.

Nearby attractions: North Fork White River, Big Spring, Bull Shoals Lake, Norfork Lake.

For more information: See the appendix for contact information.

The Drive

The Blue Buck Knob Scenic Byway passes farms and pastures in the hilly, forested Ozarks, and visits a 27-acre lake during its journey across southwest Missouri. The two-lane road is paved and has frequent turnouts. Traffic is usually light year-round.

Summers are very hot and humid with temperatures well into the 90s and humidity around 70 percent. Fall temperatures can range from the 50s to 70s with relatively low humidity. Winters are variable, but generally cold with some rain and snow. Spring is very pleasant with warming temperatures and occasional thunderstorms.

Beginning at the north end of the byway, coming from U.S. Route 60 at Cabool, take Missouri Route 181 to where it enters the Mark Twain National Forest. A sign indicates the commencement of the byway.

Pull off to the north side at Indian Creek for a scenic overlook of how this land is carved into hills and hollows, with rivers eroding deep valleys into the Ozark Plateau. Looking into the valley of Indian Creek, the rock

Drive 14: Blue Buck Knob Scenic Byway
Mark Twain National Forest

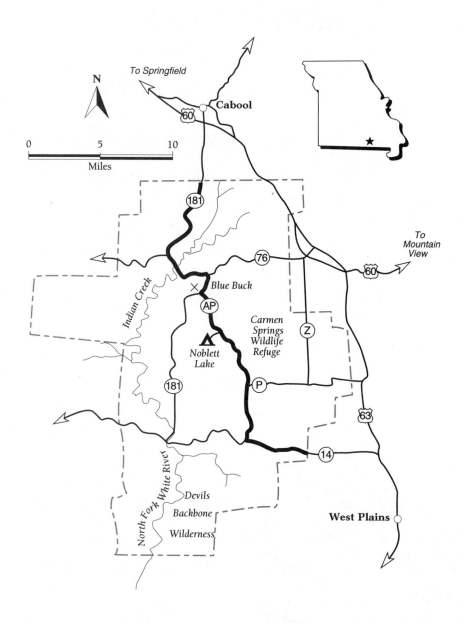

bluffs and rugged terrain are heavily forested with oak and pine.

In spring, the forest, especially along Indian Creek, is resplendent with scattered and blossoming dogwoods and redbuds, as well as understory wildflowers, including mixtures of trillium, blue bells, and dogtooth violets. Oaks and hickories provide spectacular autumn foliage. Eastern redcedar, shortleaf pine, sassafras, and the splendidly colored black gum tree highlight the fall showcase.

The Civilian Conservation Corps (CCC) constructed Blue Buck Fire Lookout Tower in the 1930s. The USDA Forest Service used it first, then the state, as a fire lookout, but now it serves only as a radio site. Take the trail a short way up the fairly rugged, but not-too-steep slope, to the tower. Enjoy a panorama of forest hills, the area's knobs, and the distant drainages of the North Fork to the south and west and Indian Creek to the north. Also, notice the mosaic of farms, open fields, and grazing areas in the lowlands. At the lookout's base, a small picnic area provides a good rest stop on your trip.

Descend from the lookout, cross Noblett Creek, and then climb back up to the turnoff for Noblett Lake. A spur road off Missouri Route AP takes you about 0.5 mile to the lake.

The CCC also constructed Noblett Lake in the 1930s. Its 27 acres are very popular for fishing, swimming, hiking, and camping. The day-use area gets a lot of use with two shelters, 13 picnic tables, flush toilets, and drinking water. You can launch your boat, hike around the lake, have a picnic, or set up camp. The Sycamore Loop Campground has ten sites just below the dam in a heavily timbered area along the creek. There are no hookups.

Ridge Runner National Recreation Trail also originates at Noblett Lake. This 20-mile linear hiking route heads south through the North Fork Recreation Area, along the ridgeline and crossing several drainages. It ends at North Fork but connects with other trails that take you through Devil's Backbone Wilderness. Aside from hiking, visitors also enjoy horseback riding, fishing for bass and bluegill, spotting a variety of Midwest songbirds, and hunting for deer and wild turkeys.

Just opposite the byway lies the Carmen Springs Wildlife Refuge, which was established in the 1930s to restore the white-tailed deer and now stocks areas throughout the state with deer from the refuge. Wild turkeys were also reintroduced to Missouri through this refuge and now there is hunting for deer and turkeys.

Pass the church at the crossroads of Oak Grove and continue south on the byway. The Ozark Trail crosses this byway at Dry Creek. Having started near St. Louis, it hooks into the Ridge Runner Trail. You'll find a parking area and trailhead right on the byway to explore this portion of the Ozark Trail and to spot the Lovers Leap bluff on the east side of the byway.

Traffic is usually light year-round on the Blue Buck Knob Scenic Byway.
MARK TWAIN NATIONAL FOREST PHOTO

Continuing south, just on the west side of the byway, there are a variety of trails that are all part of the Steam Mill Hollow Area. Specific trail information is available from the nearby ranger district office.

Although there has been quite a bit of logging, the area's reforestation process has involved planting or seeding some of the pine trees and allowing the oak trees to come back by themselves. As the byway comes to its southern terminus, the timbered slopes give way to serene farmland and pastured areas of southern Missouri. The byway ends at its junction with Missouri Highway 14 just outside of Siloam Springs.

15

Covered Bridge Scenic Byway
Wayne National Forest

General description: A 44-mile highway that winds through scenic hills and past numerous covered bridges.

Special attractions: Little Muskingum River, historic tours, Marietta riverfront and attractions, covered bridges, autumn foliage, wildflowers, wildlife.

Location: Southeast Ohio on the Wayne National Forest. The byway travels Ohio Route 26 between Woodsfield and Marietta.

Byway route number: Ohio Route 26.

Travel season: Year-round.

Camping: Five national forest campgrounds, with picnic tables, fire grates, and toilets.

Services: All traveler services in Marietta and Woodsfield. Limited services available at various communities along the byway.

Nearby attractions: Ohio River, Ohio River Museum, Campus Maritius Museum, mound cemetery, Middleton Doll Company tours, Blennerhassett Island.

For more information: See the appendix for contact information.

 The Drive

Covered Bridge Scenic Byway winds through the hilly, picturesque region of southeastern Ohio. The narrow two-lane road has a few pullouts, and traffic moves about 35 to 45 miles per hour along the twisting route. Traffic is generally light.

Summertime temperatures reach a humid 90 degrees, with thunderstorms and occasional flash flooding along the river. Fall and spring temperatures range from about the 30s to the 60s. Spring tends to be wet, and autumn is mostly sunny. Winter days reach the 40s and 50s and nighttime temperatures are below 30 degrees.

The byway is scenic driven in either direction. When driving south to north, begin in Marietta—the first non-native settlement in the Northwest Territory. Marietta was established in 1788 and has retained a rich historical flavor. Riverboat trade was a major part of Marietta's economy, and today you can tour the maritime museum to revisit the past. An attractive riverfront

Drive 15: Covered Bridge Scenic Byway
Wayne National Forest

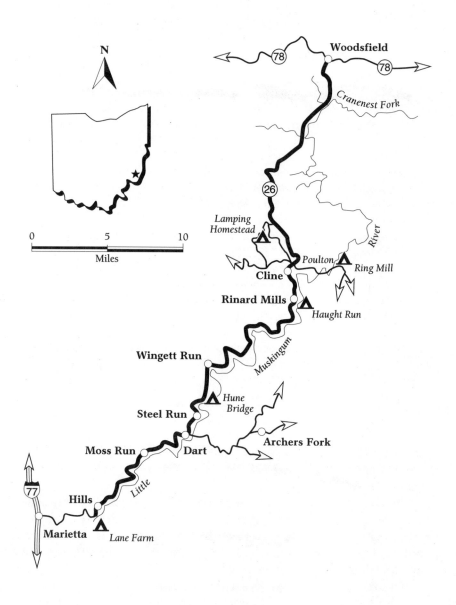

N

0 5 10
Miles

Woodsfield

78

Cranenest Fork

26

Lamping Homestead

Poulton

Cline

Ring Mill

Rinard Mills

Haught Run

Wingett Run

Muskingum

River

Hune Bridge

Steel Run

Moss Run   Dart

Archers Fork

77

Hills

Little

Marietta   *Lane Farm*

has a walking mall, red brick streets, shops, paddle wheel boat, and restaurants. The town cemetery is located around two large Indian burial mounds.

There are several historic tours around Marietta, including trolley car tours through town. During the summer months a ferry shuttles people to Blennerhassett Island in the Ohio River. The mansion built here in the 1700s has been restored, and there are tours, buggy rides, picnicking, and shopping opportunities on the island.

Other area tours include the Fenton Glass Factory and Rossi Pasta factory; historic Parkersburg, West Virginia; and the Middleton Doll Factory at nearby Belpre. The doll factory produces porcelain dolls. The factory itself looks like a giant dollhouse and is especially beautiful when lit with Christmas lights.

The byway follows Ohio Route 26 along the Little Muskingum River. This river corridor winds through some of the most picturesque rural farmland in the Midwest. Small farms and crossroad communities are interspersed with forested land. Weathered barns painted as Mail Pouch Tobacco billboards are found here, and covered bridges, over a century old, are still in use. There are a variety of recreation opportunities along the scenic byway.

Canoeing is excellent from fall through spring, and there are some nice swimming holes. The river appears muddy, and in fact, the Indian word "Muskingum" translates to mean muddy river. Fifty-two species of fish inhabit the river, including the native stream muskellunge and endangered Ohio brook lamprey. Anglers fish for smallmouth, spotted, and largemouth bass; crappie; sauger; bluegill; and catfish, among others. Chiggers, ticks, and poison ivy can be a nuisance to the unwary.

The byway winds through a region of farms and rolling hills, and you'll travel either along the river valley or up to ridgetops for extended views. American beech; sugar maple; black, white, and swamp oak; and shagbark and pignut hickory vegetate the steep slopes. Dogwood and redbud blossoms brighten the forest understory each spring.

The first covered bridge along this byway appears near the community of Hills. Nearby, Lane Farm is a small recreation area in the trees that provides opportunities to picnic, fish, and camp. There are three campsites available. Walk across the covered bridge to hike a portion of the North Country Trail. This moderate trail winds east and north from here as far as Woodsfield. The North Country Trail is a National Scenic Trail that will eventually wind through the country, linking New York and North Dakota.

Hikers are likely to see beavers, white-tailed deer, and turkeys. Other forest inhabitants include rabbits, squirrels, muskrats, red and gray foxes, minks, racoons, skunks, and opossums. The endangered river otter and bobcat also reside in this region. Bird watchers can look for endangered king rails, as well as great blue herons, Canada geese, bluebirds, warblers, vireos, and red-tailed and sharp-shinned hawks.

A typical scene along the Covered Bridge Scenic Byway.
WAYNE-HOOSIER NATIONAL FOREST PHOTO

The byway leaves the river near Moss Run, and climbs up to a good view of the ridges and drainages lying to the east and south. Continue north on the highway, and take a side trip east from Dart. Park at the North Country Trailhead and hike south about 1 mile to Archers Fork, to see a natural stone bridge. There are many scenic rock outcrops and rock formations in the area, but the most impressive is the massive rock bridge that you can actually walk across.

This is a region rich in oil and gas, with some of the oldest wells in the country. Occasionally you may see cables crossing the road, from antiquated wells connected to a pump house down by the river. If the flags are moving, the oil well is pumping. Most of the wells, however, are well hidden by vegetation.

Back on the byway, travel north past Steel Run to the Hune Bridge Recreation Area. You can drive right over this picturesque covered bridge into the camping and picnic area. There are two campsites and good access for launching a canoe on the Little Muskingum River. You can hike another portion of the North Country Trail, called the Covered Bridge Trail here, which runs from Hune north 4.5 miles to the Rinard Covered Bridge just past Wingett Run. Another recreation area at Rinard Mills, called Haught Run, provides three campsites and good river access.

The byway continues north, through pastoral, rural countryside. The Knowlton Covered Bridge is near Cline, and a small county park provides picnic facilities.

A side trip east from Cline leads about 3 miles to Ring Mill, a historic mill site. En route, the road goes right between a house and barn, so watch for chickens and cows on the road. Ring Mill is the northernmost launch point for canoeing the Little Muskingum River. There are three campsites and a picnic area. An interpretive sign explains about the Walter Ring House, which housed four generations of millers from 1846 until 1921.

Continuing north on the byway, the Lamping Homestead has picnic sites and a 5-mile loop trail. This tranquil site includes a 5-acre pond stocked with bluegill, bass, and catfish.

The byway leaves the river and follows smaller streams, climbs ridges to expansive vistas, then drops back into the valley to end at Woodsfield. This small community has a quaint rural atmosphere and some antique shops.

16

Highland Scenic Byway
Monongahela National Forest

General description: A 44-mile route through the green, rolling Allegheny Mountains, past flowing rivers.

Special attractions: Fishing, hiking, Cranberry Mountain Nature Center, camping, colorful autumn foliage, Cranberry Glades Botanical Area.

Location: Southeast West Virginia on the Monongahela National Forest. The byway begins east of Richwood and follows West Virginia Route 39/55 to the Cranberry Mountain Nature Center. From there it follows West Virginia Route 150 northeast to U.S. Highway 219.

Byway route numbers: West Virginia Route 39/55 and West Virginia Route 150.

Travel season: West Virginia Route 39/55 is open year-round. West Virginia Route 150 is open from about mid-March through mid-December and then closed by winter snows.

Camping: Three national forest campgrounds within 5 miles of the byway, with drinking water, toilets, picnic tables, fire grates, and fishing available. Numerous additional national forest campgrounds in the area.

Services: All services in Richwood and in nearby Marlinton.

Nearby attractions: Cass Scenic Railroad and historic lumber town, Pearl S. Buck Birthplace, Green Bank National Radio Astronomy Observatory, Civil War battlefields, rafting, cross-country and alpine skiing, spelunking, music and crafts festivals, Droop Mountain Battlefield, Watoga and Beartown state parks.

For more information: See the appendix for contact information.

 The Drive

The Highland Scenic Highway travels from Richwood east through wildflowers and forests and then turns north and parallels the Cranberry Wilderness border. The two-lane road is paved. Traffic on the byway is generally light, and the route has frequent viewpoints and recreational opportunities.

Summertime high temperatures average 65 to 75 degrees. Winter temperatures may drop below zero, but daytime temperatures are generally between 10 and 25 degrees. The average annual precipitation of 50 to 65

Drive 16: Highland Scenic Byway
Monongahela National Forest

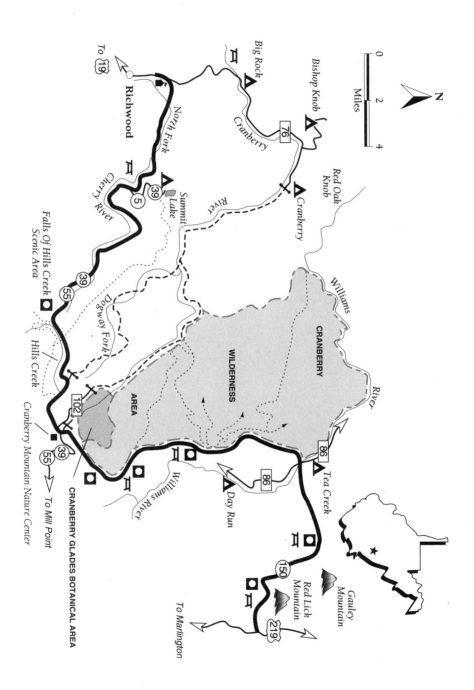

inches is relatively evenly distributed throughout the year, with snowfall averaging 120 to 140 inches a year.

Beginning at Richwood, drive east on West Virginia Route 39/55. A side road just outside of town, Forest Road 76, leads 5 miles to Woodbine Picnic Area. Nearby, Big Rock Campground has five sites. Another 6 miles on Forest Road 76 brings you to Cranberry Campground, with 30 sites. The three recreation areas are located along the Cranberry River, one of West Virginia's best trout streams.

Trout fishing along the scenic byway is some of the best in the state. Awaiting your line are brook, brown, rainbow, and golden trout. Summit Lake, the North Fork Cherry River, Williams River, and nearby Cranberry River are stocked with trout, while several smaller streams support native brook trout populations.

Throughout its length, the byway passes through predominantly hardwood forests consisting of yellow poplars, red and white oaks, sugar and red maples, beeches, yellow and black birches, black cherries, white ashes, basswoods, and others. Eastern hemlock is a common conifer, and red spruce occurs at higher elevations, sometimes in pure stands. Wildlife in the area includes black bears, bobcats, white-tailed deer, raccoons, opossums, snowshoe hares, red and gray foxes, squirrels, wild turkeys, ruffed grouse, and several species of hawks and owls as well as many songbirds.

The byway begins at the national forest boundary near the Gauley Ranger Station, which has visitor information available. North Bend Picnic Area is a pleasant stop. Just beyond it, a side trip on West Virginia Route 39/55 leads north 2 miles to Summit Lake Campground, which has 33 sites. The 42-acre lake provides opportunities for boating and fishing, including a fishing pier and a boat ramp for nonmotorized craft. An easy 1.5-miles footpath offers attractive views of the lake, and numerous other trails are nearby for more strenuous hiking through the national forest.

Back on the byway, Falls of Hills Creek Scenic Area is 16 miles east of Richwood. It features three waterfalls—25-, 45-, and 63-feet high—in the midst of rich northern hardwood forests. Footpaths and stairways lead to observation points for each of the falls.

3 miles east of the Falls of Hills Creek, the byway crosses Kennison Mountain at an elevation of 3,988 feet. It then descends into the headwaters drainage of the Cranberry River. Forest Road 102 is a side trip leading 1.5 miles north to the unique 750-acre Cranberry Glades Botanical Area. A 0.5-mile boardwalk with interpretive signs provides safe access to two of four open bogs and their associated shrub and forest communities. Numerous plants and animals that normally live far to the north can be found here.

You can drive Forest Road 102 another mile north to the gate at the boundary of the Cranberry Backcountry. Beyond the gate, the road provides

*Big Spruce Viewpoint overlooks lush wildflowers and extensive forest
along the Highland Scenic Byway.* KEN HALTENOFF PHOTO

nonmotorized access to the 26,000-acre area. Fishing is excellent in the
Cranberry River. Forest Road 102 also provides access to the Cranberry
Wilderness and its extensive system of hiking trails, and to the 7-mile
Cowpasture Trail, which circles the botanical area.

The scenic byway continues east from Forest Road 102 to Cranberry
Mountain Nature Center, located at the junction of West Virginia Route 39/
55 and West Virginia Route 150. The center offers traveler information,
exhibits and interpretive programs about local ecology and history, and natu-
ralist-led tours of the Cranberry Glades. The nature center is open from
Memorial Day through Labor Day, and weekends the rest of the year, except
for December when it is closed.

The byway turns north at the nature center and travels West Virginia
Route 150. This section of the byway is considered a parkway and managed
primarily for scenic and recreational use. Roadside camping is prohibited,
and a 45-miles-an-hour speed limit encourages leisurely recreational travel.

This portion of the Highland Scenic Highway is the highest major road
in West Virginia. Sixty percent of the road is above 4,000 feet, and more
than 88 percent is above 3,500 feet. The road forms the eastern boundary of
the 35,864-acre Cranberry Wilderness. More than 70 miles of hiking trails

provide access for hiking and backcountry camping within and near the wilderness area. Several trailheads are signed along the parkway.

In this area, the parkway passes through red spruce, hardwood, and shrub forests along the crest of Black Mountain, reaching a maximum elevation of 4,556 feet before descending to cross the Williams River at 3,038 feet. Three developed overlooks provide views of Cranberry Glades and the Williams River Valley. Another overlook, accessible by the mile-long High Rocks Trail, affords a spectacular view across the Greenbrier River Valley to the southeast.

Forest Road 86, a side road on the Williams River 13.5 miles north of the nature center, leads 1 mile north to Tea Creek Campground, with 29 sites. Day Run Campground, with 12 sites, is 4 miles south on Forest Road 86. The Williams River is a popular fishing stream for stocked rainbow, brook, and brown trout.

The parkway turns east and climbs Tea Creek Mountain and then crosses Gauley Mountain, where a trailhead provides access to more than 20 miles of hiking trails. The nearby Little Laurel Overlook provides a panoramic view of Black Mountain, Spruce Mountain, and the Williams River Valley.

On the east side of Gauley Mountain, the parkway overlooks the upper Elk River drainage, with Cheat Mountain, Buzzard Ridge, and Clovelick Mountain in the background. The parkway passes east of Red Spruce Knob and then south of Red Lick Mountain to Red Lick Overlook and Picnic Area, from which you can get expansive views of the Greenbrier River Valley. The route descends gradually to U.S. Highway 219 at an elevation of 3,525 feet on Elk Mountain, 7 miles north of Marlinton.

—Ken Haltenhoff

17

Longhouse Scenic Byway

Allegheny National Forest

General description: A 29-mile loop through beautiful hardwood forests and around Kinqua Bay on the Allegheny Reservoir.

Special attractions: Allegheny National Recreation Area, autumn colors, lake recreation, wildlife watching, bicycling, hunting, cross-country skiing, snowmobiling, camping.

Location: Northwest Pennsylvania on the Allegheny National Forest. The byway travels a triangle—Pennsylvania State Highway 321 from Bradford Ranger Station south 11 miles to the junction with Forest Road 262; Forest Road 262 from its junction with Pennsylvania State Highway 321 northwest to its junction with Pennsylvania State Highway 59 near Morrison Bridge; and Pennsylvania State Highway 59 from Morrison Bridge east to Bradford Ranger Station.

Byway route numbers: Pennsylvania State Highway 321, Forest Road 262, Pennsylvania State Highway 59.

Travel season: Pennsylvania State Highway 321 and Pennsylvania State Highway 59 open year-round. Forest Road 262 closed by snow from about mid-December through March.

Camping: Three national forest campgrounds along the byway, with picnic tables, fire grates, flush toilets, showers, drinking water, playground, and dumping stations. Numerous public and private campgrounds within 30 miles of the byway.

Services: Traveler services in Bradford, Kane, and nearby Warren and Sheffield. Gas, boats, bait, snacks, some lodging, and meals available at various places along or near the byway.

Nearby attractions: Allegheny State Park, National Seneca Iroquois National Museum, Kinzua Bridge State Park, Hickory Creek Wilderness, Lake Chautauqua State Park and Institute, Knox, Kane, Kinzua Railroad.

For more information: See the appendix for contact information.

 The Drive

The Longhouse Scenic Byway winds through hardwood forests atop a large plateau and along an arm of Allegheny Reservoir. The two-lane route is paved and has frequent scenic turnouts. Traffic moves slowly and is moderate

Drive 17: Longhouse Scenic Byway
Allegheny National Forest

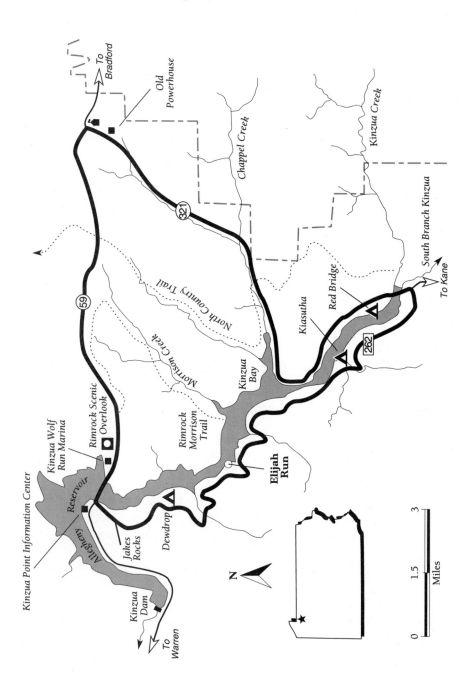

from spring through fall. Forest Road 262 is not maintained in the winter.

Summer daytime temperatures average about 80 degrees; spring and fall range from about 40 to 70 degrees. Rainfall is moderate. Winter sees plenty of snow, with average temperatures ranging from about 10 to 40 degrees.

The byway is very scenic driven in either direction. Begin at the Bradford Ranger Station, where you can obtain national forest information and maps.

The Allegheny Mountains are part of the Appalachian Mountain chain. This region was once under an ocean, but movements of the earth's crust pushed up the mountain chain. The limestone from the ocean was compressed into shale, which trapped rich pockets of oil and natural gas.

The mountains are generally flat-topped and covered with a lush growth of hardwoods. Rivers and streams have cut steep channels into the mountains and exposed interesting rock outcrops. The dense forest is predominately black cherry, maple, northern red oak, beech, aspen, and white oak.

About 0.5 mile south of the ranger station you can see a working oil well at the old powerhouse. The highway follows North Fork Creek, then Chappel Creek. Chappel has a nice fishery of native and stocked rainbow trout.

The North Country National Scenic Trail crosses the byway about 5 miles from the ranger station. This 85-mile trail crosses the entire national forest from north to south. Stretch your legs and sample a few miles of the trail by hiking north up a small mountain for the reward of several nice views over the Allegheny Reservoir. A good half-day hike takes you about 7 miles north to the Pennsylvania State Highway 59 portion of the scenic byway.

The Allegheny National Forest has a variety of wildlife, including at least 49 mammal species. Most abundant are rabbits, squirrels, turkeys, grouse, white-tailed deer, and black bears. Raptors such has hawks, osprey, and eagles soar overhead, while great blue herons can often be seen fishing along the banks of streams and the reservoir.

The byway travels along Chappel Bay, providing several nice views of the reservoir through the screen of trees. Allegheny Reservoir encompasses 7,634 acres on the upper Allegheny River. In addition to generating power, the reservoir offers numerous recreation opportunities to camp, fish, boat, watch wildlife, and swim.

Red Bridge Campground has 55 sites nestled in a large grove of maple and white pines. Many of the sites are right near the water.

Boating is very popular on the Allegheny Reservoir and you'll likely see people fishing, water-skiing, and sightseeing from the water. Boats can be rented at the marina.

Turn northwest onto Longhouse Scenic Drive (Forest Road 262) at the

Longhouse Scenic Byway encircles part of the Allegheny Reservoir, seen here from Rimrock Scenic Overlook. ALLEGHENY NATIONAL FOREST PHOTO

National Forest Scenic Byway sign about 11 miles from the Bradford Ranger Station. This section of the byway twists and turns and rolls up and down the hills and valleys. The speed limit is 35 m.p.h. In places, the road travels right along the edge of the reservoir; other times it climbs as much as a thousand feet above the water. There are several boat ramps along the route and numerous places to park off the road and walk down to the reservoir for bank fishing.

Kiasutha Campground provides 90 sites in the forest. Look for delicious blackberries around the campground in August. There is a picnic area, boat launch, and beach. Evening naturalist programs are presented in summer at the amphitheater. Hikers can walk a 1-mile-long interpretive trail and learn about natural resources, trees, and wildlife.

Elijah Run boat ramp has been renovated for people with disabilities, with an accessible fishing pier, restrooms, and a paved walkway. It also has a great view across the water to Morrison Campground, which is accessible only by boat or on foot. Just past Elijah Run, another pullout offers a scenic view down the whole southern stretch of the Kinzua Arm.

Dewdrop Campground has 74 sites in the dense forest. Some sites are next to the water. Nearby, follow the short paths at Jake's Rocks Scenic Overlook to look down more than a thousand feet to the reservoir. This is the highest point along the scenic byway.

Cullasaja Falls in the Nantahala National Forest in North Carolina. PHOTO BY LAURENCE PARENT

The Longhouse Scenic Byway through Allegheny National Forest in Pennsylvania. PHOTO BY JIM SCHWABEL/NEW ENGLAND STOCK

The Rinard Covered Bridge near Marietta, Ohio in the Wayne National Forest.
PHOTO BY ROGER BICKEL/NEW ENGLAND STOCK

*Top: Sunset from Eagle
Overlook in the Kisatchie
National Forest in Louisiana.*
PHOTO BY LAURENCE PARENT

*Bottom: Brilliant autumn
color along the
Appalachian Trail as it
winds its way through
New Hampshire and the
White Mountain National
Forest on its way to
Maine and Georgia.*
PHOTO BY ROBB HELFRICK

A view from an overlook in the Ozark National Forest. PHOTO BY LAURENCE PARENT

Seneca Rocks in the Monongahela National Forest in West Virginia.
PHOTO BY GERRY BROOME

A historic ranger residence in Pisgah National Forest in North Carolina.
PHOTO BY LAURENCE PARENT

Upper Kiamichi River Wilderness in the Ouachita National Forest in Oklahoma.
PHOTO BY LAURENCE PARENT

Endless ridges in the Chattahoochee National Forest in northern Georgia. PHOTO BY ROBB HELFRICK

Along the Talimena Scenic Byway in the Ouachita National Forest in southeastern Oklahoma. PHOTO BY JIM ARGO/PHOTOGRAPHIC RESOURCES

Cross-country skiing in Nicolet National Forest in northern Wisconsin.
PHOTO BY MICHAEL SHEDLOCK/NEW ENGLAND STOCK

Trout fishing in the area along the Mount Rogers Scenic Byway in Virginia's Jefferson National Forest is considered some of the best in the southern Appalachians. PHOTO BY LAURENCE PARENT

About 0.5 mile past Jake's Rocks another spectacular view is presented. The large oak trees at the overlook frame Morrison Bridge and the reservoir to the north. It's a photographer's delight.

The byway continues north to its junction with Pennsylvania State Highway 59. The Kinzua Point Information Center has interpretive displays explaining area history and uses of the national forest and Allegheny Reservoir. You can talk to staff about the area and obtain maps, brochures, and interpretive materials.

A side trip west on Pennsylvania State Highway 59 goes to the community of Warren, which has traveler services. Cross the river and go back east if you would like a self-guided tour of the Allegheny Fish Hatchery.

Kinzua Dam has two viewing places: one atop the dam and one at the bottom. An information center at Big Bend presents videos and explains the workings of the dam.

The byway travels east on Pennsylvania State Highway 59, crossing Morrison Bridge across the upper arm of Kinzua Bay to a marina, boat ramp, and picnic area. The Rimrock Scenic Overlook provides yet another great view from atop a big rock outcrop, across the reservoir.

The byway rolls through the hardwoods atop the plateau. The abundant white pines and hemlock trees of this region were heavily logged and nearly wiped out in the latter 1800s. They left the hardwoods, and today the Allegheny National Forest has dense, mature forests of fine hardwoods such as black cherry, maple, ash, and oak. Autumn foliage is absolutely breathtaking, and in June the mountain laurel blossoms are beautiful. Other understory plants include striped maple, blackberries, and blueberries.

Rimrock Morrison Trail winds 10.8 miles from the byway through the forest, to Morrison Boat Camp. You could choose a shorter 5.3-mile cutoff loop to enjoy strolling through this beautiful forest. Wear waterproof boots for the many stream crossings. About 2 miles farther east, North Country Trail crosses Pennsylvania State Highway 59. The byway reaches its eastern terminus at Bradford Ranger Station.

18

Kancamagus Scenic Byway

White Mountain National Forest

General description: A 34-mile paved road through the heart of the White Mountains.

Special attractions: Brilliant autumn foliage, trout fishing, swimming, skiing.

Location: Central New Hampshire on the White Mountain National Forest, north of Laconia. The byway travels New Hampshire Route 112 between Lincoln and the junction of New Hampshire Route 112 and New Hampshire Route 16.

Byway route number: New Hampshire Route 112.

Travel season: Year-round. Expect winter driving conditions from November through May.

Camping: Six national forest campgrounds with drinking water, picnic tables, fireplaces, and toilets. No hookups. Campgrounds open mid-May through early to mid-October except for Blackberry, Big Rock, and Hancock, which are open all year. The last two are plowed during the winter. There are numerous additional national forest campgrounds within a short drive of the byway.

Services: All services in Bartlett, Lincoln, Conway, and North Conway.

Nearby attractions: Old Man of the Mountain; Clark's Trading Post; Mount Washington; ski areas; Conway Scenic Railroad steam-train ride; and Presidential Range-Dry River, Sandwich Range and Pemigewasset wilderness areas.

For more information: See the appendix for contact information.

 The Drive

The Kancamagus Highway climbs from Lincoln, elevation 811 feet, to an altitude of 2,855 feet in its first 10 miles. Then it slowly descends the remaining 18 miles through a variety of outstanding scenery. The two-lane highway is paved and has numerous turnouts, and traffic can be heavy depending upon the season. Kancamagus Highway is considered one of the best highways in the United States from which to view fall foliage.

The weather is extremely variable, which is typical for New England. Spring can be rainy, or the byway may still be wrapped in snow and cold into May. Generally, summer visitors will experience temperatures as high

The Kancamagus Highway winds 28 miles through the heart of the White Mountains.
WARREN B. MCGRANAHAN PHOTO

as the low 90s, but plenty of shaded areas and cool mountain breezes keep the drive comfortable.

The town of Lincoln, at the western end of the byway, caters to the traveler. Loon Mountain and Cannon Mountain ski areas have attracted many top-quality gift shops that are open year-round.

The byway follows the Swift River and the East and Hancock branches of the Pemigewasset River. The Swift River is stocked with brook and rainbow trout, and fishing is both popular and rewarding. Most stretches can be fished without waders either by moving from rock to rock or by taking advantage of the river's delightful summer temperatures and simply wading in shorts.

The name "Kancamagus" comes from a famous New Hampshire Indian who began his rule as chief of the Penacook Confederacy in 1684. History relates that Kancamagus tried to encourage peace between the Indians and the whites until harassment from the English aggravated him too much and he retaliated. When the confederate tribes scattered in 1691, Kancamagus and his followers moved either to northern New Hampshire or into Canada.

East of Lincoln, Loon Mountain Recreation Area offers skiing and a year-round gondola ride. There is a nature trail at the top of the mountain, and the view is excellent.

Drive 18: Kancamagus Scenic Byway
White Mountain National Forest

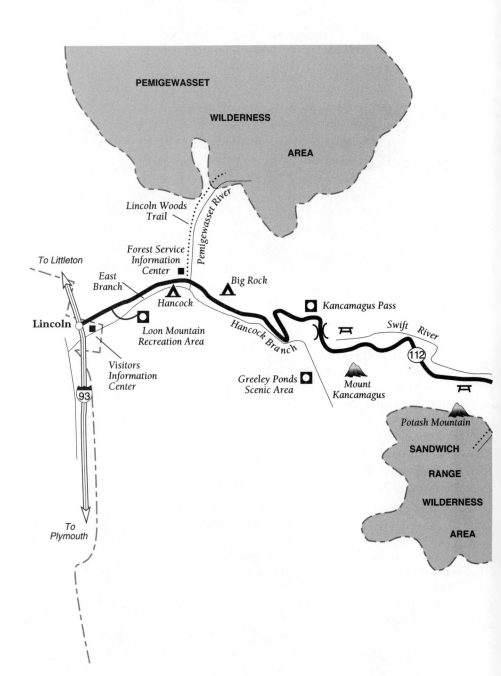

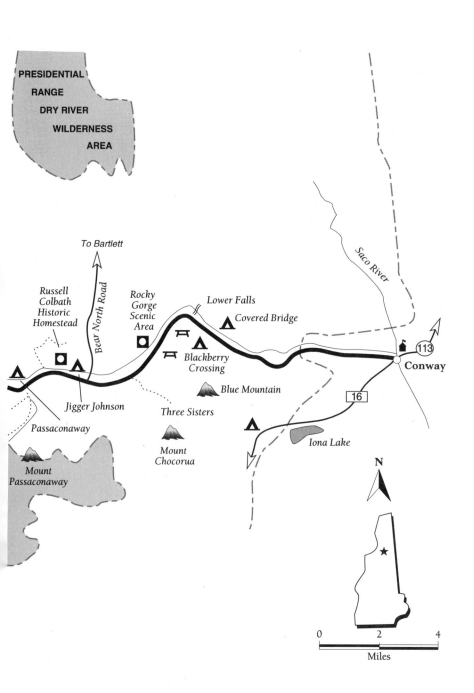

PRESIDENTIAL
RANGE
DRY RIVER
WILDERNESS
AREA

Saco River

To Bartlett

*Russell
Colbath
Historic
Homestead*

*Rocky
Gorge
Scenic
Area*

Lower Falls

Covered Bridge

Bear North Road

*Blackberry
Crossing*

Jigger Johnson

Blue Mountain

Passaconaway

Three Sisters

113

Conway

16

*Mount
Chocorua*

Iona Lake

*Mount
Passaconaway*

N

0   2   4
Miles

Hancock Campground, situated in a beautiful birch stand, has 56 sites, running water and flush toilets, fishing, and hiking.

Almost 5 miles east of Lincoln on the byway is the popular Lincoln Woods Trail, which leads into the Pemigewasset Wilderness. The trail parallels the East Branch of the Pemigewasset River. It is a very popular and easy hike that follows an old logging railroad bed. Hikers are offered views of the river and will see old logging ties. The log cabin visitor's center also serves as a cross-country ski center and elementary school educational center in winter.

The byway travels alongside the Hancock Branch of the Pemigewasset River and climbs to Big Rock Campground, which has 28 sites adjacent to the river. The campground was named for the large rock just inside its entrance. Swimmers enjoy dipping in Upper Lady's Bath, a five-minute walk from the campground.

Scenic overlooks permit frequent stops to admire the scenery. The area is ablaze with bright foliage in autumn. Each bend in the road reveals a new montage of yellows, reds, and oranges vividly splashed against the ever-constant green of stately spruces and hemlocks. Off to the north are the Pemigewasset and the Presidential Range-Dry River wilderness areas. The Presidential Range-Dry River Wilderness features distinctive geologic formations and mountain peaks varying in elevation from 3,000 to 4,000 feet. The Appalachian Trail, a National Scenic Trail, runs along the northern and western boundaries. Hardwoods occupy the lower slopes; mixed birches, maples, spruces, and firs the middle slopes; and spruces and firs the upper slopes. Portions of the major ridges are above timberline and are dotted with typical "krummholtz" vegetation. Wildlife habitat is not as diverse in the wilderness, although deer, black bears, grouse, hares, and a variety of birds associated with high mountain slopes are found.

There are three mountains over 4,000 feet within or on the edge of the Pemigewasset Wilderness: Mount Hancock, Mount Bond, and Owl's Head. Major attractions of the area are trails along the long, gentle valley bottoms, constant views of adjacent streams, and isolation.

Most exposed mountains are granitic, based on Paleozoic Plutonic bedrock formations. The Passaconaway Gravel Pits hold smoky quartz crystals, and other area mountains yield magnetite, tin, and adularia feldspar.

Greeley Ponds Scenic Area can be reached via a 1.5-miles hike over forest trails.

The C.L. Graham Wangan Ground has picnicking and a nice view. The headwaters of the Swift River emerge from Lily Pond, and the byway follows the deep cleft the river has carved into the rock over the years. Wangan ground is an Indian term for meeting place.

White-tailed deer, moose, black bears, grouse, raccoons, weasels, squirrels, and a variety of songbirds inhabit the byway region.

Passaconaway Campground has 33 sites, fishing, and hiking. The UNH Trail is a moderately strenuous 5-mile hike that leads to the open ledges on the summit of Hedgehog Mountain for views of the Sandwich Range.

A short distance farther along the byway is the Passaconaway or Albany Intervale, a parcel of rich, flat land first settled about 1790. The Russell-Colbath House, listed in the National Register of Historic Places, is located here.

The Rail 'n' River Hike follows an easy 0.5-mile trail that begins at the historic house. Self-guiding interpretive points along the trail tell the story of the changes in the landscape.

Jigger Johnson Campground has 76 sites located on the intervale. A side trip on Bear Notch Road allows you to explore the surrounding area.

Champney Brook Trail winds an easy 1.5 miles to the falls, which are spectacular in the spring and after heavy rains but somewhat meager in dry seasons. Champney was a pioneer White Mountain artist. Another path goes about 200 yards beyond Champney Falls to the base of Pitcher Falls, which is seasonal also.

Farther east along the byway, the Swift River has worn a cleft in the rock. The area is now known as Rocky Gorge Scenic Area. Within this area is Falls Pond, a five-minute walk on a graded path that crosses the gorge via a rustic footbridge. A trail circles the pond. Lower Falls, a short distance below Rocky Gorge, is a popular swimming area.

Covered Bridge Campground has 49 sites along the river. The Boulder Loop Trail is also located near the campground. It is less than 3 miles long, and its gradual climb is interrupted occasionally by steep pitches. This 3-mile interpretive trail tells the story of the formation of soils in the area and the origin and growth of the forest. There are several good views of Mount Chocorua and the Swift River from the ledges along the trail.

Across from Covered Bridge, Blackberry Crossing Campground has 20 sites. Remains of an old Civilian Conservation Corps (CCC) camp are still visible.

The byway continues east along the Swift River and ends in Conway, at the junction of New Hampshire Route 112 and New Hampshire Route 16.

—*Warren B. McGranahan*

19

Highlands Scenic Tour

George Washington National Forest

General description: A 20-mile loop tour through stream valleys and along a ridgetop overlooking the Allegheny Highlands and Blue Ridge Mountains.

Special attractions: Rich Hole Wilderness, historic mines, spring blossoms, autumn foliage, far-ranging vistas, fishing, hiking.

Location: West-central Virginia on the George Washington National Forest. The byway travels Virginia State Highway 850 north from Longdale Furnace (Interstate 64æExit 10) to its junction with Forest Road 447 (Interstate 64æExit 11); Forest Road 447 south to its junction with Star Route 770; and Route 770 west to Longdale Furnace.

Byway route numbers: Virginia State Highway 850 (formerly U.S. Highway 60), Forest Road 447, and Star Route 770.

Travel season: Year-round on Virginia State Highway 850. Star Route 770 and Forest Road 447 occasionally closed by winter ice and snows, usually between December and early March.

Camping: No national forest campgrounds on the byway.

Services: All traveler services in nearby Clifton Forge and Lexington.

Nearby attractions: Rough Mountain Wilderness, Longdale Recreation Area, Lake Moomaw, Appalachian Trail, Blue Ridge Parkway, downhill ski areas, Douthat State Park, Natural Bridge and Caverns, Virginia Horse Center, Highland National Forest Scenic Byway (West Virginia).

For more information: See the appendix for contact information.

 The Drive

The Highlands Scenic Tour travels through diverse vegetation and historic mining country, providing beautiful views and access to a wilderness area. Virginia State Highway 850 is a paved two-lane road. Forest Road 447 and Star Route 770 are narrower, two-lane gravel roads. Star Route 770 is steep with hairpin turns, not recommended for large RVs or towed units. Traffic is usually light to moderate on the byway.

Summer daytime temperatures average in the 70s to low 80s and nights cool down to the 50s or 60s. Winter days usually climb to the 50s and may drop to freezing at night. Most of the region's 38 inches of annual precipitation

Drive 19: Highlands Scenic Tour
George Washington National Forest

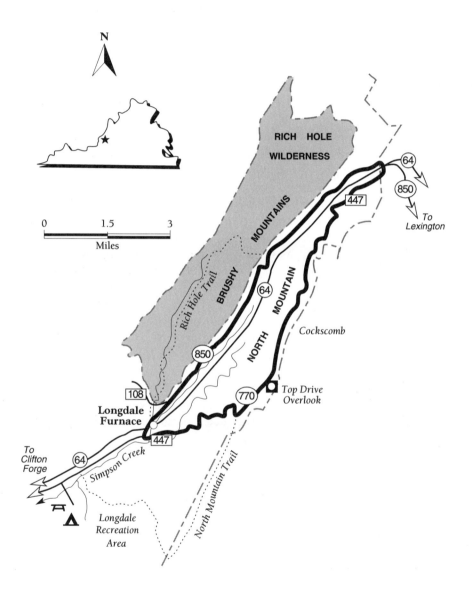

comes from spring and summer thunderstorms.

Beginning your tour in Longdale Furnace, evidence of the 19th Century pig iron industry remains. The two tall chimneys still standing are remnants of the Lucy Selina Furnace, now registered under Virginia Historic Landmarks.

A few miles west, Longdale Recreation Area was the site of a busy Civilian Conservation Corps (CCC) camp in the 1930s. It has a small lake with a swimming beach, bathhouse, picnic sites, and an easy walking trail.

The byway follows two nearly parallel routes in its loop. Virginia State Highway 850 is the paved "low road" along Simpson's Creek and Bratton's Run. This narrow valley is steep and has lush vegetation. Brushy Mountain, containing the Rich Hole Wilderness, fills the western horizon. This wilderness protects 6,450 acres of streams and hardwoods on Brushy Mountain. The forest is composed primarily of red, white, and scarlet oaks; tulip poplars; white pines; dogwoods; hemlocks; and sugar, red, and silver maples.

Down along the creek, pockets of rhododendrons brighten the stream banks with their spectacular springtime blossoming. Blossoming dogwood, redbud, sourwood, and mountain laurel usually peak in mid- to late-April along this low road, and peak in early- to mid-May along the high road.

Take a side trip north on Forest Road 108 to the Rich Hole Wilderness trailhead. This 5.9-mile moderately strenuous footpath traverses the wilderness and ends back out on the highway. Have one person shuttle the car and pick you up at the other end. The trail follows the cascading waters of North Fork Simpson Creek through stands of big poplars, oaks, and hickories. A unique feature for this region is a large stand of old hemlock. The creek has native brook and rainbow trout. There are occasional views east to the Shenandoah Valley. From the ridgetop, you'll see west into Rough Mountain Wilderness, before descending back to the byway.

Wildlife in this region includes black bears, white-tailed deer, wild turkeys, ruffed grouse, and squirrels. Look for beaver dams along Simpson Creek. Bird enthusiasts may hear the songs and calls of mockingbirds, robins, cardinals, warblers, wrens, nuthatches, flycatchers, and kingfishers. Red-tailed hawks and buzzards soar overhead.

Simpson Creek valley has abundant reminders of the mining industry. The Allegheny Highlands were an important source of pig iron in the late 1700s and throughout the 1800s. Iron for Confederate Army ammunition came from this region during the Civil War. Remnants of building foundations, bridge abutments, and mine entrances remain. A narrow gauge, or "dinky," railroad ran from the Langdale iron mine to furnaces in the valleys, and you can still make out the terrace for railroad tracks carved into the sidehill. Streams still run red from the iron oxidizing at abandoned mines, but the charcoal hearths and brick foundations are now covered in vegetation.

The Highlands Scenic Tour winds through the forest atop North Mountain, providing views of the Shenandoah Valley and Blue Ridge Mountains.
GEORGE WASHINGTON NATIONAL FOREST PHOTO

The forest was clearcut to make charcoal and has now regenerated. Some of this can be viewed from the road but is more likely to be seen by taking short walks through the valley.

The byway continues northeast, passing the northern trailhead for the Rich Hole Trail. George Washington National Forest covers 1,055,000 acres and extends 140 miles along the Appalachian Mountains, in Virginia and West Virginia. There are more than 800 miles of hiking trails.

The byway descends along Bratton's Run (which has good fishing for native brook trout), leaves Virginia State Highway 850, crosses under Interstate 64, and follows Forest Road 447 south. You'll climb North Mountain via a series of hairpin turns. Occasional vistas open up to the west, into Rich Hole Wilderness and beyond to the Allegheny Highlands. The road crosses the ridge and follows the eastern side of North Mountain, providing great views over the Shenandoah Valley.

The forest here is primarily oaks, walnuts, and tulip poplars. Rhododendrons and mountain laurels adorn the ridgetop. Spring blossoms and fall foliage are stunning. The bright yellows, oranges, and reds of autumn foliage usually peak in mid- to late-October.

After traveling about 4.5 miles on Forest Road 447, you can get out of your car for a short, ten-minute hike up to a vertical rock outcrop called Cockscomb. This is a 0.3-mile, fairly steep trail leading to a terrific view. It's worth the effort. About 1.5 miles farther south on the byway, Top Drive Overlook provides another spectacular panoramic view of the area.

Highlands Scenic Byway traverses the ridge and valley physiographic region characteristic of the Appalachian Mountain Range. Steep-sloped, parallel ridges run southwest to northeast, with long, narrow valleys between. Here, the Blue Ridge Mountains are to the east and the Allegheny Highlands to the west.

To extend your appreciation of the big vistas, hike the North Mountain Trail. It follows the crest of North Mountain about 4 miles, then drops down another 4.6 miles to Longdale Recreation Area. It's an excellent hike, well worth your time.

The scenic byway completes the loop returning to Longdale Furnace on Star Route 770. A large turnaround area at Top Drive Overlook permits RVs and cars towing trailers to return via Forest Road 447 to avoid the steep, switchbacking hairpin turns on Star Route 770.

Star Route 770 is a charming road, lined with stone retaining walls built more than 150 years ago by prisoners and slaves. It was constructed to transport charcoal, from Collierstown on the east side of North Mountain to the furnaces on the west side of the mountain. Charcoal was necessary to process the iron ore. Star Route 770 is one of the oldest roads in use in the Commonwealth of Virginia, and the quality of craftsmanship is outstanding.

20

Big Walker Mountain Scenic Byway

Jefferson National Forest

General description: A paved, 16-mile open loop around and up Big Walker Mountain.

Special attractions: Trout fishing, southern Appalachian hardwood forest, wildflowers, diverse wildlife, scenic views, camping, hiking trails, historical Civil War site.

Location: Southwest Virginia on the Jefferson National Forest, northwest of Wytheville. From Wytheville, head northwest on Interstate 77, exiting at Exit 52 onto Virginia Route 717. The byway travels west on Virginia Route 717 to its junction with U.S. Highway 52 and then follows U.S. Highway 52 back north and east to Interstate 77.

Byway route numbers: Virginia Route 717 and U.S. Highway 52.

Travel season: Year-round.

Camping: One national forest campground with bathhouses, picnic tables, fire grates, and drinking water.

Services: No services on the byway. All services in nearby Wytheville.

Nearby attractions: The Appalachian Trail, Mount Rogers Scenic Byway and National Recreation Area, Wytheville State Fish Hatchery, Rock House Museum in Wytheville.

For more information: See the appendix for contact information.

 The Drive

The Big Walker Mountain Scenic Byway, nestled in the southwestern arm of Virginia, is bordered by century-old stands of white pines, as well as southern Appalachian hardwoods such as oaks, hickories, hemlocks, chestnuts, redbuds, dogwoods, and a mix of Virginia, pitch, and table mountain pines.

The byway ranges in elevation from 2,500 feet at each end to 4,000 feet at the Big Bend Picnic Area. Summers are hot, humid, and often rainy and overcast, with temperatures reaching 90 degrees. Fall temperatures are moderate, and there are extensive periods of rain and cloud cover. Winter is snowy, and the thermometer dips into the teens. Spring brings sunny days in the 50s and 60s.

From early spring through mid-July, you can see rhododendrons, mountain laurels, and wild azaleas in bloom. The forest explodes with other

Drive 20: Big Walker Mountain Scenic Byway
Jefferson National Forest

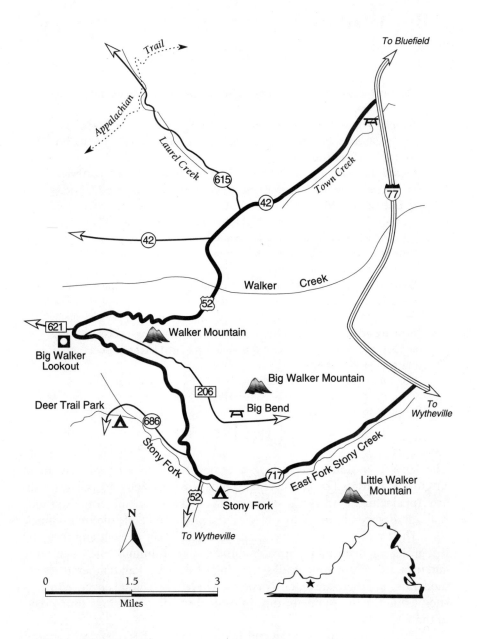

To Bluefield

Trail

Appalachian

Laurel Creek

615

42

Town Creek

77

42

Walker   Creek

52

621

Walker Mountain

Big Walker
Lookout

Big Walker Mountain

Deer Trail Park

206

Big Bend

To
Wytheville

686

Stony Fork

717

East Fork Stony Creek

Little Walker
Mountain

52

Stony Fork

N

To Wytheville

0   1.5   3
Miles

wildflowers, such as pink and yellow lady slippers, native orchids, and lo-- belias. Forest inhabitants include white-tailed deer, wild turkeys, grouse, groundhogs, squirrels, cardinals, robins, blue jays, and a variety of song- birds.

Once the bottom of the ocean, the area is primarily sedimentary rock, with large deposits of sandstone. The southern slopes of Big Walker and Little Walker mountains are gentle, while the northern slopes are quite steep and many strata are exposed. The soils, especially along Stony Fork Creek, are fertile but rocky. Early settlers devoted a great deal of time to rock re- moval before they could plant. At best, the soils supported kitchen gardens and limited grazing.

Settlement took place as early as the 1740s. This was the frontier, and Indians subjected settlers, building on traditional hunting lands, to frequent raids. Big Walker and Little Walker mountains were considered prime hunt- ing lands, with plentiful deer and bear. Several tribes fought pitched battles for the right to hunt this section. The Shawnee likely were victorious. Ar- chaeological explorations have uncovered numerous Shawnee artifacts.

The byway is an open loop and can be traveled in either direction. If you start the byway tour from the junction of Interstate 77 and Virginia Route 717, you will travel in a clockwise direction. About 1 mile from the

Travelers on Big Walker Mountain Scenic Byway enjoy far-ranging views over the rolling hills, fields, and forests of southwest Virginia. JEFFERSON NATIONAL FOREST PHOTO

beginning of the byway is the trailhead for the Seven Sisters Hiking Trail (also open to mountain bikes). The trail is 4.3 miles long and terminates at Stony Fork Campground.

Just beyond the side road is the Astin homesite. Ollie and Buck Astin lived here and raised a family from the early 1900s through the 1970s. They cut pulp wood for sale, skidded logs with horses and mules, dug ginseng, and fed themselves and their children by cultivating a large garden and hunting wild game. All that remains of the homestead are the posts of an old pen, some fruit trees, and an overgrown blackberry patch. Deer can frequently be observed feasting on the berries.

Stony Fork Campground lies about 4 miles from the beginning of the byway. There are 53 sites and a trailer dump station nearby. A nature trail forms a 1-mile loop, and the trees and flowers along the way are identified. The East Fork of Stony Fork Creek runs through the campground, offering fishing, wading, and wildlife-watching opportunities. There are rainbow trout and panfish varieties such as sunfish and pumpkinseed fish in the creek.

Just beyond the campground, turn north onto U.S. Highway 52. A side trip on Virginia Route 686 leads west to Deer Trail Park Campground. The byway climbs Big Walker Mountain, ascending from 2,500 feet to 3,700 feet in less than 3 miles. Dry Gulch Junction, the skeleton of a defunct western-theme park, is on the east. Deer are often seen moving through the tall grass past the boarded-up buildings.

Forest Road 206 makes a sharp intersection with the byway; the turn is difficult for large motor homes to navigate. The route leads 4 miles east to Big Bend Picnic Area, constructed in the 1930s by the Civilian Conservation Corps (CCC). From here, you have a view of the ridge and valley terrain to the south. There are picnic tables, grills, and fireplaces scattered in the orchard grass under a canopy of oaks. Vault toilets are provided.

Back on the byway, Big Walker Lookout is a privately owned 100-foot fire tower open to tourists for a fee. A platform to the right of the tower offers a magnificent view of the valley and surrounding ridges. A nearby plaque commemorates Toland's Raid and Molly Tynes. Colonel Toland commanded a force of Union troops bivouacked near Tazewell, Virginia, during the Civil War. It was common knowledge that he and his men planned to cross the mountains and capture the railroad depot at Wytheville. Young Molly Tynes took it upon herself to ride over the mountains and warn the citizenry of the impending raid. With no Confederate troops in the area, a group of Home Guards—older men, young boys, and a few women—turned out to defend the position. They repulsed the Union forces and killed Colonel Toland during the battle.

West of the lookout, the Walker Mountain Trail provides a 1-mile hike along the crest of Big Walker Mountain. This trail provides good views of the valley below.

About 3 miles down the mountain from the lookout, a historical marker notes the home site of S.H. Newberry, a member of the "Big Four" in the Virginia Senate. It was this group that put an end to an influx of carpetbaggers and helped Virginia recover financially from the Civil War.

The byway traverses rolling fields planted in crops or used for grazing horses and cattle. Virginia Route 615 leads north to provide access to the Appalachian Trail. There are 79 miles of the Appalachian Trail within this ranger district. The byway ends at the intersection of U.S. Highway 52 and Interstate 77.

—Barbara Elliott

21

Mount Rogers Scenic Byway

Jefferson National Forest

General description: A 55.5-mile paved highway through the scenic forests and countryside surrounding Mount Rogers, highest point in Virginia.
Special attractions: Mount Rogers National Recreation Area, the Appalachian Trail, Lewis Fork and Little Wilson Creek wilderness areas, historic logging towns.
Location: Southwest Virginia on the Jefferson National Forest, south of Marion. Mount Rogers Scenic Byway is divided into two parts: 23 miles of Virginia Route 603, from Troutdale southwest through the center of Mount Rogers National Recreation Area to the intersection with U.S. Highway 58; and 32 miles of U.S. Highway 58, from Damascus east to Volney, along the south edge of the Mount Rogers National Recreation Area.
Byway route numbers: U.S. Highway 58 and Virginia Route 603.
Travel season: Year-round.
Camping: Seven national forest campgrounds with individual sites and one campground with group sites. All have picnic tables, fire grates, toilets, drinking water, and trailer dumping stations. No hookups.
Services: Lodging, store, food, and gas in Damascus. Gas and convenience store in Troutdale and Konnarock. All services in nearby Marion, Abingdon, and Bristol.
Nearby attractions: Hungry Mother State Park, Grayson Highlands State Park, Barter Theatre in Abingdon, Salt Mine Museum, and numerous regional festivals.
For more information: See the appendix for contact information.

 ## The Drive

The Mount Rogers Scenic Byway winds through forested areas and open countryside. Portions of U.S. Highway 58 are unsuitable for vehicles or trucks more than 35 feet long. The byway has moderately heavy traffic, with July and August the busiest months. The two-lane, paved route is lined by a diversity of established private farms and the more recently dedicated forest land set aside in 1966 for public recreational activities. The entire Jefferson National Forest encompasses more than 702,000 acres of valleys and rolling hills of the Blue Ridge Mountains.

Summer visitors can expect daytime temperatures of about 75 degrees, with nights in the 50s to 70s. Spring and autumn range from about 40 to 70 degrees, and winter temperatures may rise to 60 or plunge well below freezing.

Virginia Route 603 begins at Troutdale, where a population of 3,000 once thrived during the area's logging boom of the early 1900s. Troutdale was the home of author-publisher Sherwood Anderson, and the dwelling is now a historical monument open to visitors. Quietly reminiscent of its earlier heyday, Troutdale is a pleasant stopover as well as a good restocking point for campers in need of supplies.

The forest is composed of typical eastern hardwoods, such as maples, oaks, walnuts, poplars, ashes, and locusts. Alpine meadows often sprout Fraser firs and red spruces.

A multi-use area located in 4-mile-long Fairwood Valley is at about 3,500 feet in elevation. Within this strikingly beautiful stretch of open pasture, wildflowers bloom year-round, horses and cattle graze, and fruit trees entice pickers to harvest their seasonal crops. Many miles of trails are devoted to the enjoyment of hikers and horseback riders.

Prior to 1900, Fairwood was the site of a large residential community of employees and officials of the Hassinger Lumber Company. Once a part of that community, the Fairwood Livery now offers seasonal horse rentals for rides into the high country of Pine Mountain (elevation 5,000 feet). One of the trails, the Virginia Highlands Horse Trail, provides 67 miles of riding paths and is accessible from the byway 4 miles west of Troutdale. Nearby is Fox Creek Horse Camp, a camping area for those who bring their own horses.

The next 2 miles of byway will pass several trailheads. The Lewis Fork Wilderness Trail lets hikers and cross-country skiers enjoy the seasonal variations of the forested landscape year-round. A third trailhead, 6 miles west of Troutdale, offers another path into the Lewis Fork Wilderness and connects with trails to Mount Rogers, the highest peak in Virginia at 5,729 feet. The mountain is noted for its open meadows, abundant wildflowers, and extensive summit cover of spruces and firs.

In all, there are 450 miles of multi-use trails in the byway area for hiking, bicycling, skiing, and horseback riding. The Appalachian Trail crosses the scenic byway three times and covers about 60 miles in the byway area.

Trout fishing in this byway area is some of the best in the southern Appalachians. There are native brook trout and stocked varieties of brook and rainbow trout. Thirty-five streams on the national forest are designated for native brook trout, and about 150 miles of streams have mixed trout species. Warm-water fishing for striped and largemouth bass is good in South Holsten Reservoir, just south of the byway. The New River on the east end of Mount Rogers National Recreation Area is considered excellent for smallmouth bass fishing.

Drive 21: Mount Rogers Scenic Byway

Jefferson National Forest

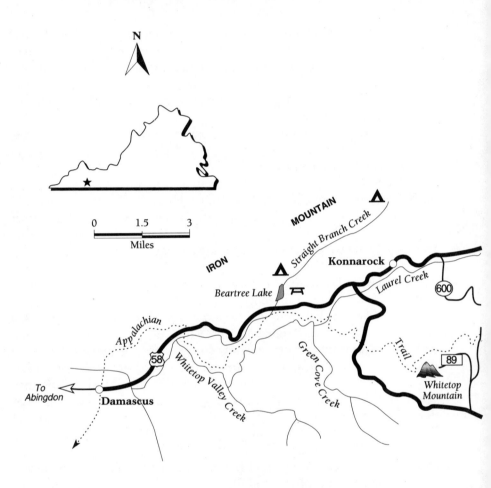

Grindstone Campground has 108 sites and restrooms with showers. Also featured are a 400-seat amphitheater, the Whispering Waters Nature Trail, and several other paths that connect with the Appalachian and Mount Rogers trails. Other activities include swimming, trout fishing, and horseback riding.

Several miles west of Grindstone Campground, a side trip south on Virginia Route 600 and then west on Forest Road 89 leads to the summit of Whitetop Mountain. Whitetop derives its name from the snow or frost that sometimes covers its summit. From the summit, at 5,500 feet, you will have a spectacular view of Mount Rogers and vicinity. The landscape is unusual

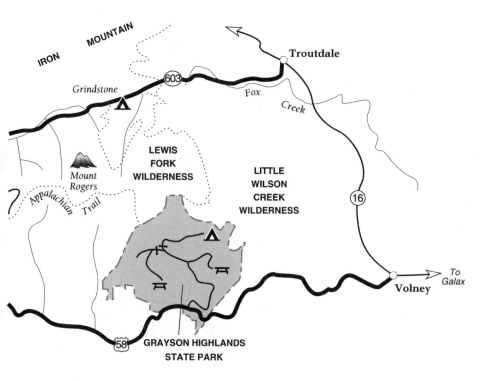

because it is the divide between geologic formations that show evidence of volcanic action, as well as oceanic and coastal sedimentation. Glaciation, continental uplift, and erosion are evident in the area.

Returning to the byway, you can replenish camping supplies in Konnarock. Historically reminiscent of the logging boom is the Lutheran Girls School, built during the late 1880s by the Hassinger Lumber Company. The school provided board and education for the daughters of loggers. Completely sided with chestnut bark, the school has weathered many years. It remained operational until the 1960s. The lumber mill remains, and period residences and a Lutheran church made entirely of stone are all historic attractions of this community.

This portion of the byway ends at the junction of Virginia Route 603 and U.S. Highway 58. The second segment of byway is on this adjacent stretch of U.S. Highway 58, between Damascus and Volney.

Beginning at Damascus, the byway winds through a mixed hardwood forest and pastures as it skirts the southern flanks of Whitetop Mountain, visible from various points along the route. The route parallels much of Straight Branch Creek, which provides good fishing. You can see portions of the old Virginia Creeper Railroad bed, now a National Recreation Trail that provides easy hiking and bicycling.

Beartree Campground features a lake with picnic facilities, swimming, boating, and fishing. The campground has 90 individual sites and eight group sites. Wildlife viewing is a popular pastime. You may enjoy locating beaver ponds and watching the animals' busy routine. Other animals on the Jefferson National Forest include deer, foxes, turkeys, grouse, opossums, racoons, and skunks.

Grayson Highlands State Park is located near the terminus of the scenic byway, near Volney. This park provides good, year-round access to the high country of the Mount Rogers National Recreation Area, and it features seasonal cultural events that are regionally popular.

—*Ken Haltenhoff*

Hikers on the Virginia Creeper National Recreation Trail cross this scenic railroad bridge in Mount Rogers National Recreation Area. KEN HALTENHOFF PHOTO

22

Zilpo Road

Daniel Boone National Forest

General description: A 9.1-mile road across forested ridges and hollows to Cave Run Lake.

Special attractions: Colorful autumn foliage, hiking and horseback trails, an old fire tower, blossoming shrubs, diverse wildlife, examples of timber-harvesting methods and wildlife-management practices, wildflowers.

Location: Eastern Kentucky on the Daniel Boone National Forest, east of Mount Sterling. The byway travels the entire length of Forest Road 918. To find it, follow Kentucky Route 211 south of U.S. Highway 60, turn east onto Forest Road 129, and follow the signs for Zilpo Campground.

Byway route number: Forest Road 918.

Travel season: Year-round.

Camping: Two national forest campgrounds with drinking water, toilets, picnic tables, and fire grates. Campgrounds open from mid-April to mid-October. Select units have hookups.

Services: All services in Morehead. Gas, telephone, and food in Salt Lick.

Nearby attractions: Clear Creek Recreation Area, Sheltowee Trace National Recreation Trail, Cave Run Lake, Red River Gorge Geological Area, Minor Clark Fish Hatchery, Natural Bridge State Park, Tater Knob Fire Tower.

For more information: See the appendix for contact information.

 The Drive

Lying within the northern half of the Daniel Boone National Forest, the byway meanders a little more than 9 miles across forested ridges and hollows and around hills before ending at the entrance gate to the Zilpo Recreation Area. There are a few sharp curves and steep grades along the route.

Crisp mornings, sunny days, and cool evenings characterize spring weather. There are occasional thunderstorms, but for the most part the weather is pleasant. Daytime temperatures can reach the mid-60s, and nighttime lows in the 20s are not unusual. Summer temperatures are often in the upper 80s, and humidity levels can be high. Fall weather is similar to that of spring. Typical winter temperatures are in the 20s, and 2 to 6 inches of snow is the average.

Drive 22: Zilpo Road
Daniel Boone National Forest

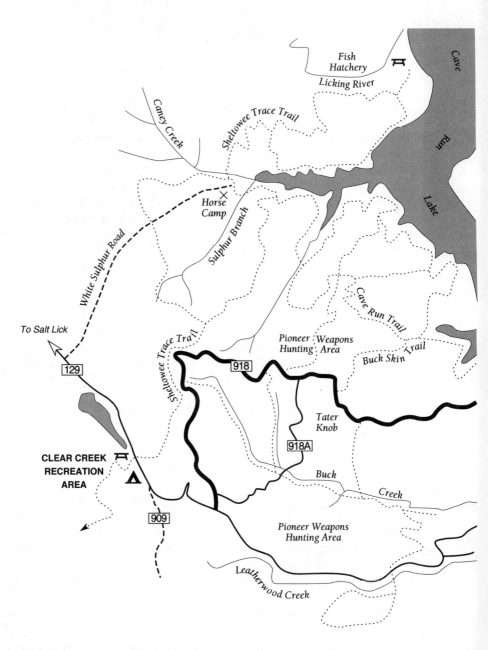

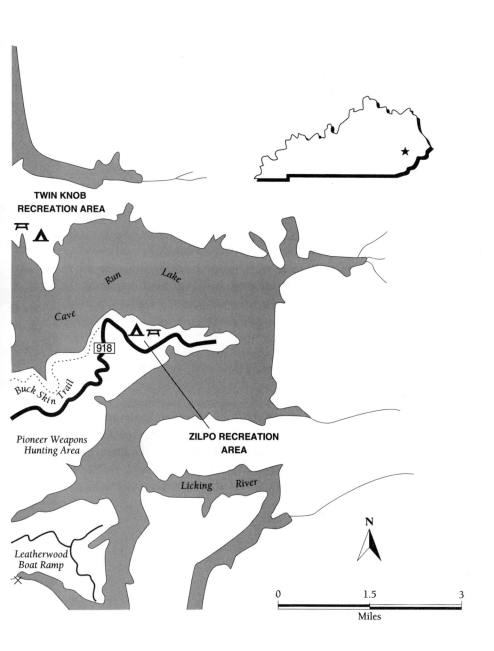

TWIN KNOB
RECREATION AREA

Run   Lake

Cave

918

Buck Skin Trail

Pioneer Weapons
Hunting Area

ZILPO RECREATION
AREA

Licking   River

Leatherwood
Boat Ramp

N

0   1.5   3
Miles

The southern hardwood forest consists of oaks, yellow poplars, hickories, redbuds, dogwoods, maples, beeches, scattered clumps of pines, sycamores, and occasional black walnuts. In the autumn, the varied reds, oranges, and golds of changing leaves make for excellent color viewing. In spring, the redbud and dogwood blossoms are striking.

You may see white-tailed deer feeding along ridge tops and in hollows. The best time for viewing wildlife is around sunrise or sunset. Deer are relatively abundant in this part of the national forest, and hunting is a popular activity.

In addition to deer, look for red foxes, groundhogs, rabbits, skunks, squirrels, wild turkey, geese, wood ducks, mallards, grouse, ospreys, hawks, owls, and a variety of songbirds.

The ridges are composed of Newman limestone over a thick bed of siltstone, all covered with a shallow layer of soil. The hollows are transported soils and siltstone carried from higher elevations by area streams.

The Zilpo area has a rich history of Indian settlement. Banks of flint are abundant, and there are signs that early Indians worked their tools here. As in all national forests, no artifacts may be removed.

Clear Creek Lake and Recreation Area is located on Forest Road 129 near the beginning of the byway. The 43-acre lake is stocked with large-mouth bass, channel catfish, and sunfish. There is also a boat launch, and the lake is perfect for canoeing. Only electric motors are permitted.

Situated around the lake are nesting boxes for wood ducks and nesting platforms for Canada geese. The USDA Forest Service is establishing a resident goose flock, and a large number of banded geese are present. Wood ducks nest between March and May, geese between March and July.

The Clear Creek Iron Furnace is also part of the recreation area. Though only the crumbling stone stack remains today, the furnace was once the site of frenzied activity. Each summer between 1839 and 1857, the furnace, built to smelt pig iron, gobbled up huge amounts of surrounding forest to keep running. The environmental impact of these logging practices was catastrophic, even in that day and age.

In contrast to the way the iron furnace was fed are today's methods of harvesting timber. The first interpretive stop on the byway details modern timber-harvesting techniques and how they are used as a tool for wildlife management, providing browse for deer, berries for ruffed grouse, and cover for wild turkeys.

Just beyond the first overlook, the byway enters the Pioneer Weapons Hunting Area. In season, hunters may hunt this area only with bow and arrow, crossbow, flintlock, or percussion cap rifle. Many hunters use the old forest roads in the vicinity for foot travel during the season. The roads and trails are also open to backpackers, horseback riders, mountain bicyclists,

Interpretive sites complement the scenery along Zilpo Road. BARBARA ELLIOTT PHOTO

and cross-country skiers. Hikers using the area during hunting season should wear fluorescent orange for safety reasons.

Another interpretive site features a trailhead and wildlife enclosure. The trail, which is about 100 yards long, intersects the Sheltowee Trace, a 254-mile-long National Recreation Trail. Sheltowee means "Big Turtle" in the Shawnee language. The tribe gave this name to Daniel Boone when it adopted him, and the trail was named in honor of Boone, who explored the land over which it passes.

Just after the trails intersect, a fenced plot keeps wildlife out. Here trees and plants are protected so wildlife biologists can compare vegetative utilization by deer and estimate browsing pressure.

The next interpretive site on the byway is called "A Rest in the Forest." A short trail meanders through the forest to a simple wooden bench. Sunlight filtering through the leaves, the buzz of bees, and the odor of decaying leaves all serve to highlight the regenerative powers of the forest on the mind and soul.

Sitting atop the next ridge is the Tater Knob Fire Lookout Tower, one of the highest points in the area at elevation 1,388 feet. The tower was manned from 1932 until the early 1970s and is the last remaining tower on the Daniel Boone National Forest. You can visit between sunrise and sunset for three seasons, but it is closed in winter.

Leaving Tater Knob, the road dips into a hollow and climbs to the summit of the next ridge and overlook. A panoramic view includes forested lands running down to the shores of Cave Run Lake, a large portion of the lake itself, and a section of the byway as it curves around a hill.

Cave Run Lake holds largemouth bass, bluegills, crappies, catfish, and an excellent muskellunge fishery. There are two marinas on the lake to serve boaters. Numerous coves are host to the many houseboats that ply the waters of the 8,270-acre impoundment. Swimmers enjoy two beaches, including the sand beach at the Zilpo Recreation Area. The lake is home to the Cave Run Sailing Association, which sponsors of several regattas each season.

The Zilpo Scenic Byway ends at the gates of Zilpo Campground and Recreation Area. The campground has 196 sites spread over 355 acres of trees and brush. Each site has a lantern holder. Water is available at centrally located sites, and there are ten bathhouses with hot showers—five of them solar-heated. Select sites have electricity.

Zilpo has a small country store, beach, hiking trails, boat ramp, and picnic area.

—*Barbara Elliott*

23

Ocoee Scenic Byway
Cherokee National Forest

General description: A 26-mile route past a lake and through the rock bluffs of the Ocoee River Gorge, with a side trip up Chilhowee Mountain.
Special attractions: White-water rafting, excellent fishing, lakes, hiking trails.
Location: Southeast Tennessee on the Cherokee National Forest, east of Cleveland. The byway follows U.S. Highway 64 on national forest lands between Cleveland and Ducktown, and it includes Forest Road 77, a spur road from U.S. Highway 64 north to Chilhowee Recreation Area.
Byway route numbers: U.S. Highway 64 and Forest Road 77.
Travel season: Year-round. Roads can be extremely icy in winter.
Camping: Two national forest campgrounds with showers, restrooms, picnic tables, and water. One with a trailer dumping station and one with electrical hookups. Campgrounds open April 4 through mid-November.
Services: All services in Cleveland. Marina, food, phone, and lodging at Lake Ocoee and Ducktown, plus several small grocery stores with gas along U.S. Highway 64.
Nearby attractions: Red Clay State Park, Hiwassee State Scenic River, Appalachian Mountains.
For more information: See the appendix for contact information.

 The Drive

Ocoee Scenic Byway was the first designated national forest scenic byway in the nation. U.S. Highway 64, two-lane and paved, winds through the Ocoee River Gorge, and the byway includes a spur trip up Chilhowee Mountain on Forest Road 77 to Chilhowee Recreation Area. Vistas from several turnouts are exceptional. Traffic on U.S. Highway 64 can be heavy, particularly in the summer. Elevations range from 838 feet at Lake Ocoee to 2,200 feet at Chilhowee Recreation Area.

Summer visitors can expect variable weather, with temperatures ranging from the mid-70s to the mid-90s. The area is humid and has an average annual rainfall of 52.6 inches.

Cleveland, 15 miles west of the byway, is a mostly industrial city of 29,400 people. Driving east from Cleveland, your view includes Big Frog

Drive 23: Ocoee Scenic Byway

Cherokee National Forest

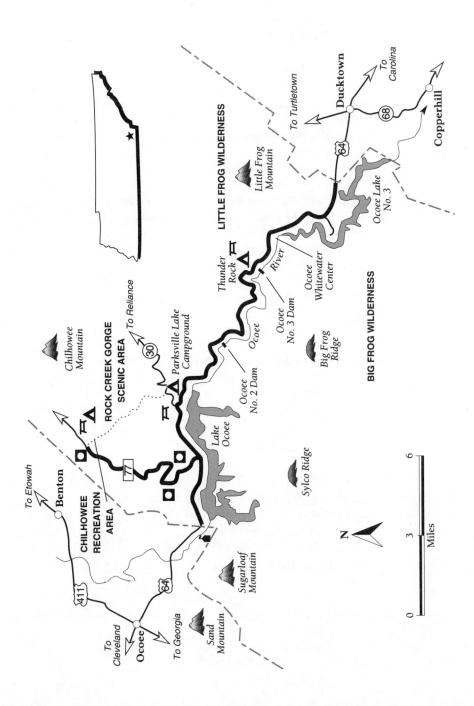

Mountain in the background and Chilhowee and Sugarloaf mountains in the foreground. The first overlook is on the dam that creates Ocoee, also called Parksville Lake. The 1,950-acre lake is entirely surrounded by national forest. It has a marina, swimming beaches, campsites, a boat launch, fishing, hiking trails, and drinking water available.

Ocoee Inn and Marina has boat gas, food, phone, and lodging. Nearby Parksville Beach, at the lake's edge, offers restrooms, open grassy areas and shady benches.

About midway down the lake, just east of the Ocoee Ranger Station, you can turn north on Forest Road 77. A steady 3-mile climb leads through a forest of shortleaf and Virginia pines; scarlet, chestnut, and red oaks; dogwoods; maples; sourwoods; and black locusts. As this spur road climbs Chilhowee Mountain, the views change from tunnel-like corridors to magnificent vistas. Parksville Lake, Sugarloaf, and Gazebo overlooks afford you views that stretch more than 40 miles west across the Tennessee Valley to the Cumberland Mountains and 15 miles south into the Cohutta Mountains of Georgia. Parksville Lake Overlook has a short loop trail that provides an opportunity for easy day hiking. Sugarloaf Overlook has barrier-free picnic tables.

A visitor to Chilhowee Overlook 125 years ago could have witnessed armies marching toward one of the most decisive conflicts of the Civil War at Chattanooga. A sign at this overlook provides more information. A Civil War interpretive site, where evidence of an 1865 skirmish was found, is also along this spur road. Farther along, you will find Gazebo Overlook, built by the Civilian Conservation Corps (CCC) during the Depression. The overlook provides shelter from which to look out toward Benton.

The Chilhowee Recreation Area has a large campground with 88 sites. There is a small lake for fishing and swimming, a picnic area, amphitheater, and hiking and bicycling trails. The 0.5-mile Forest Walk Interpretive Trail leads through this area rich in Cherokee Indian history. Other trails lead to Benton Falls, and one passes the edge of the Rock Creek Gorge Scenic Area.

Hikers should be on the lookout for wildlife. Some of the more commonly seen animals are white-tailed deer, black bears, raccoons, opossums, beavers, wild turkeys, chipmunks, and squirrels.

Flora in the Chilhowee area includes pink lady slippers, sky-blue dwarf irises, white wood anemones, pink-tinged trailing arbutuses, rhododendron, mountain laurel, and bright red berries of Jack-in-the-pulpits.

Numerous elongated ridges with intervening valleys characterize the area traversed by the Ocoee Scenic Byway, all trending in a northeast to southwest direction. This is the result of folding and fracturing that took place during a mountain-building episode 230 to 260 million years ago. The rocks are metamorphic and most visible in the gorge section of the byway.

Rafters prepare to launch on the whitewater stretch of the Ocoee River, adjacent to the Ocoee Scenic Byway. DAN COOK PHOTO

Returning to U.S. Highway 64, continue east and take advantage of several scenic pullouts along the lake. There is a boat ramp, picnicking, swimming beaches, drinking water, and toilets at Mac Point. The highway then enters the Ocoee River Gorge. The rock cliffs make a striking background for the Ocoee River, a premier location for white-water rafting and kayaking from late March until early November and the site of the 1996 Olympic canoe and kayak competitions. The byway through the gorge is very congested on summer weekends.

The 6-mile gorge section of the byway is characterized by rock outcrops, cliffs, and colorful foliage in autumn. The road is quite narrow, but has some pullouts for safe viewing of the natural features and for watching river activities. Continuing east, the byway passes a rafting put-in and a flume line diversion dam.

The Tennessee Valley Authority No. 3powerhouse is located just east of the rafting take-out point near Thunder Rock Campground. Tennessee Power Company constructed a hydroelectric power complex in the gorge around 1912, TVA took it over in 1939, and the entire complex is now on the National Register of Historic Places. Look for the flume that snakes its way around the bluffs of the gorge for almost 5 miles.

Upon leaving the gorge, the byway passes another powerhouse. A large pipe that carries water through an underground tunnel from a reservoir tucked into the mountains more than 2 miles away feeds this one. The byway passes the dry streambed of the Ocoee River on the south and the Little Frog Wilderness on the north. Boyd Gap has an overlook from which you can see the Big Frog Wilderness Area.

Ducktown and Copperhill, both linked to the copper-mining industry of the past, are located on the eastern end of the byway. The old Copper Road through Ocoee River Gorge was completed in 1853 and used for transporting the high-grade ore in horse-drawn wagons to the railhead in Cleveland. The ore was the primary source of copper for the Confederacy during the Civil War. A smelter in the vicinity of Ducktown and Copperhill was established in 1878 and is now a museum. From the museum, you can see lunarlike Copper Basin. In the distance is Copperhill and the more modern smelter's stacks. The background mountains are on the Chattahoochee National Forest in Georgia.

—Dan Cook

24

Overhill Skyway

Cherokee and Nantahala National Forests

General description: A winding, 44-mile paved route through the southern Appalachian Mountains, through the ancestral territories of the Cherokee Indian nation. This route is also called the Cherohala Skyway.

Special attractions: Three wildernesses: Bold River Gorge, Citico Creek, and Joyce Kilmer Slickrock; whitewater sports, scenic overlooks, nature trails, camping, hunting, backpacking, bicycling.

Location: Southeast Tennessee and southwest North Carolina on the Cherokee and Nantahala national forests. The byway begins on Tennessee State Highway 165 near Tellico Plains, Tennessee and continues through Beech Gap on the state border (now North Carolina Route 143) to Robbinsville, North Carolina. The Overhill Skyway National Forest Scenic Byway is also called the Cherohala Skyway when referred to by the Federal Highway Administration.

Byway route numbers: Tennessee State Highway 165 and North Carolina Route 143.

Travel season: Year-round. Occasional temporary closures due to snow or ice.

Camping: Two campgrounds with toilets, drinking water, fire rings.

Services: All services in Tellico Plains and Robbinsville.

Nearby attractions: Ocoee National Forest Scenic Byway, Ocoee Whitewater Center, Great Smoky Mountains National Park, Coker Creek Village, Fort Loudoun, L and N Depot and Railroad Museum, Englewood Textile Museum.

For more information: See the appendix for contact information.

 # The Drive

The Overhill Skyway originates in the Great Valley of Tennessee and traverses the Unicoi Mountain Range during its journey across the southern Appalachian Range in Tennessee and North Carolina. The two-lane road is paved and has frequent turnouts and overlooks. Weekends along the entire byway are generally busy. Weekends in spring, summer, and fall are extremely busy along the popular Tellico River and parking can be difficult to find.

Summer visitors can expect variable weather, with temperatures ranging from the mid 70s to the mid 90s. The area is humid and has an average annual rainfall of 52.6 inches.

The southern Appalachians are composed of some of the oldest exposed rocks in the world, from the Precambrian and the Paleozoic ages. About 200 million years ago the collision of continents forced these mountains upward, during what is now known as the Appalachian orogeny. The skyway offers unparalleled views of the southern Appalachians.

Ancient Cherokee trading routes crossed these "Over the Hill Mountains," also known over the years as Enemy Mountains, and White, or Smoky Mountains. Today's citizens celebrate the connection with an annual week-long wagon train trek between Robbinsville and Tellico Plains.

These mountains and valleys have been inhabited or visited for 11,000 years. They are the ancestral home of the Cherokee Indians, who by the time of European exploration and settlement had developed sophisticated social and political systems, with agricultural economies based on corn, squash, and beans. About 22,000 Cherokees lived in about 80 towns in the southern Appalachians, with the heart of the Cherokee Nation in this Overhill region. Most of the Cherokees were forced out and marched to Oklahoma in 1838 on the infamous and tragic Trail of Tears.

Beginning in Tellico Plains, drive east on Tennesee State Highway 165, past the 1840s "Iron Foreman's Mansion" built during the extensive iron mining and smelting boom. The Cherokee Iron Works foundry was operated by Indians, then taken over by white settlers, and later destroyed during the Civil War. Stop at the interpretive display at the national forest boundary to pick up brochures and a map of the Overhill Skyway.

The route meanders alongside the Tellico River. Watch for osprey fishing in the river, as well as numerous waterfowl. The Tellico River is popular for trout fishing, canoeing, and kayaking.

At the turn of the century, lumber companies over harvested the mountains. Erosion and grazing contributed to deteriorating conditions. Beginning in 1911 and continuing through the 1950s, most of these lands were acquired for public ownership, and forest restoration begun. The Tellico River Ranger Station has a museum for visitors, and a delightful loop trail that show different artifacts of the Civilian Conservation Corps' (CCC) work to revegetate and reclaim the area in the 1930s and '40s. Tellico Ranger Station is the oldest CCC camp in Tennessee.

Oosterneck is a canoe and kayak take-out point for the Tellico River, and trout fishing is very popular.

East out Forest Road 210, Bald River Falls cascades 100 feet onto the rocks. Pheasant Field Trout Rearing Pool raises a large variety of trout and you can walk through parts of this state trout hatchery to see the operation.

Virginia pines, and climax northern hardwoods and coniferous forests

Drive 24: Overhill Skyway

Cherokee and Nantahala National Forests

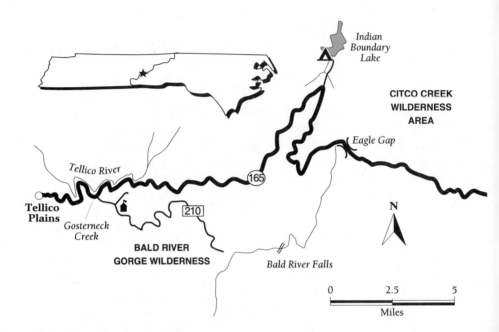

cover the mountains. Wildflower enthusiasts should watch for scarlet monarda, turk's-cap lily, large-flowered trillium, showy orchid, and squirrel corn. The treeless high ridges and mountain tops are known as balds, which may be treeless but do harbor interesting, hardy plant life. Cool mountain bogs may harbor swamp pink, and the fascinating, carnivorous pitcher plant. On high mountain ridges grow rhododendron thickets that shelter Small's twayblade, as well as other rare plants.

Bears, wild boars, deer, and northern flying squirrels inhabit the woods. You'll likely hear one of the 14 species of frogs that inhabit the national forest; their vocalizations vary from clacking to bleating to croaking.

Indian Boundary Lake was so-named because in 1819 this was the final western boundary for Cherokee lands. Indian Boundary Campground has 100 sites on the shores of the 90-acre lake, a picnic area, and a 3-mile bicycle trail. You'll find great swimming, boating, fishing, and picnic areas.

Unicoi Turnpike crosses the Overhill Skyway at several points. This historic aboriginal route begins where the Great Indian Warpath leaves the Little Tennessee River, passes south near today's Belltown and Tellico Plains

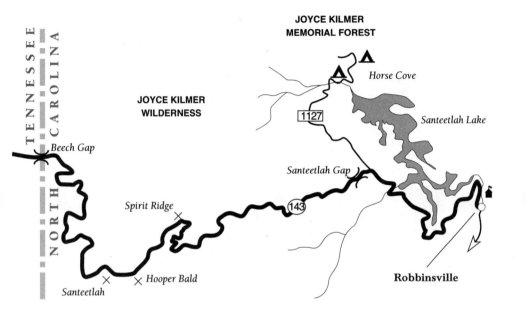

and ends at the junction of Monroe and Polk counties in Tennessee, and Cherokee County in North Carolina.

Overhill Skyway borders three exceptional natural areas: the Citico Creek Wilderness, the Joyce Kilmer Slickrock Wilderness, and the Snowbird Creek Wilderness Study Area. Beech Gap allows clear vistas into all three areas. Only the well-prepared hiker should head into the wilderness, even for a day hike. Weather conditions can change quickly.

You'll cross the state line into North Carolina through Beech Gap, elevation 4,490 feet. The byway is now on North Carolina Route 143. Take a 1-mile walk on Stratton Ridge, around "ghost" buildings of an early settlement and one grave that straddles two states. There are picnic tables, restrooms, and nice views.

The skyway's highest point is Santeetlah, at 5,390 feet. You can picnic here, at the highest overlook on the entire byway. Nearby, on Hooper Bald (elevation 5,429 feet), a 0.25-mile hike leads to views worth the effort. This once was a hunting preserve for George Moore, who imported exotic species such as Russian boars.

The Overhill Skyway traverses the Unicoi Mountain Range during its journey across the southern Appalachian Range in Tennessee and North Carolina.
CHEROKEE NATIONAL FOREST PHOTO

Driving east to Spirit Ridge, take the 0.3-mile wheelchair-accessible path through the forest to one of the most spectacular views in the southern Appalachian Mountains. Or stop for a picnic on Santeetlah Gap and browse the interpretive displays there.

The byway ends at the junction of North Carolina Routes 143 and 1127, just north of Robbinsville. A few miles north on North Carolina Route 1127, Horse Cove Campground provides 13 sites, and nearby Rattler Ford has reservation-only group camping. Joyce Kilmer Picnic Area is small, located at the entrance to the Joyce Kilmer Memorial Forest, one of the few remaining virgin hardwood forests in the Appalachians. Some trees are more than 20 feet around at the base.

25

Mountain Waters Scenic Byway

Nantahala National Forest

General description: A 61.3-mile paved route through the southern Appalachian Mountains, with whitewater river gorges, hardwood forests, and rural farm country.

Special attractions: Deep river gorges, waterfalls, broad vistas, camping, hiking, whitewater rafting, picnicking.

Location: Southwest North Carolina, on the Nantahala National Forest between Highlands and Almond. Beginning in Highlands, follow U.S. Highway 64 to Franklin, turn onto Old U.S. Highway 64, then along State Route 1310 to U.S. Highway 19, ending at the intersection of U.S. Highway 19 and North Carolina Route 28 southwest of Bryson City.

Byway route numbers: U.S. Highway 64, Old U.S. Highway 64, State Route 1310 (Wayah Road), U.S. Highway 19.

Travel season: Year-round. Occasional snow and ice in winter may require four-wheel drive.

Camping: One national forest campground open from about April through October, with picnic tables, flush toilets, drinking water, and fire grates. No hookups.

Services: All services in Highlands, Franklin, and Bryson City.

Nearby attractions: Blue Ridge Parkway, Great Smoky Mountain National Park, Cherokee Indian Reservation, Joyce Kilmer Memorial Forest, Great Smoky Mountains Railway.

For more information: See the appendix for contact information.

 The Drive

The Mountain Waters Scenic Byway traverses beautiful mountain terrain during its journey across North Carolina. The two-lane road is paved and has frequent turnouts for scenic viewing or recreation access. Traffic can be very heavy on summer and fall weekends, as well as on holidays, with the recreation season usually running from mid-April to Labor Day.

Western North Carolina has four distinct seasons. Summers and winters are moderate. Even the hottest months seldom reach the 90s. But watch for sudden and severe thunderstorms during late summer. Foliage is most colorful during the middle of October. Winter brings occasional snow and

Drive 25: Mountain Waters Scenic Byway
Nantahala National Forest

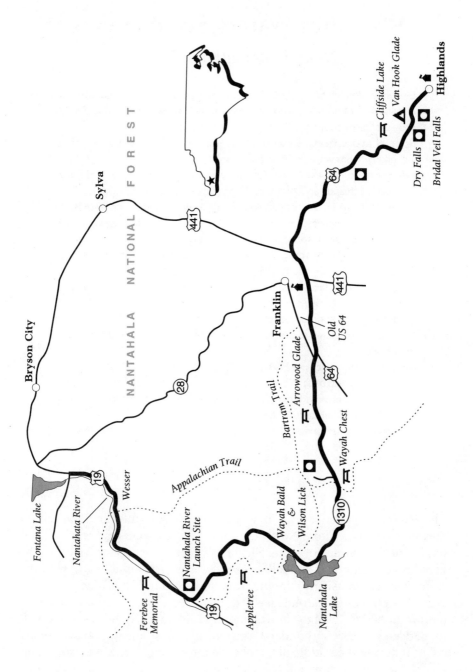

ice, but storms are usually short-lived. The area is actually considered a temperate rainforest.

Beginning at the national forest boundary northwest of Highlands, U.S. Highway 64 winds through the dramatic Cullasaja River Gorge with 14 waterfalls. Three picturesque waterfalls are well worth a stop. Bridal Veil Falls cascades in delicate, thin rivulets over the stony cliff, and you can actually drive behind it. The whole family will be entertained by walking behind 75-foot Dry Falls. The short, paved trail provides access for viewing a waterfall from the back. It's mesmerizing to stand so close and watch the stream current ebb and pulse slightly, creating ever-changing streamers of water. Cullasaja Falls drops 250 feet over the rugged rock of the gorge. There are a few pullouts around the falls area, but many of them are limited in space. From the car, you can see some of the falls through cuts that are maintained along this very narrow road.

Streamside vegetation includes flowering rhododendrons, a magnificent sight in springtime. The dense hardwood, white pine, and hemlock forest shelters inhabitants such as the black bear, red fox, grouse, turkey, and smaller animals like groundhogs and squirrels that you'll only see as they scurry beneath the underbrush.

The autumn colors in this gorge will knock your socks off—plan to stroll and gaze as long as you possibly can.

Van Hook Glade provides 20 campsites in the trees, supplied with fire grates, drinking water, and flush toilets. A very short side trip leads to Cliffside Lake Recreation Area, great for swimming, picnics, fishing for stocked trout in the summer, and hiking. Good family hikes include about 7 miles of a variety of trails: one circles the lake, others climb higher.

The scenic byway departs the river gorge and heads through pastoral countryside. You can take the four-lane bypass around Franklin, or go into town to get supplies and see the sights, including a stop at the Scottish Museum. The area around Franklin is considered the gem capital of the East, with many people hunting for rubies, amethysts, sapphires, and other hard, mineral-type stones. The Wayah Ranger Station, on Sloan Road, is a good source of information about the surrounding national forest and nearby activities.

Six miles from Franklin, exit U.S. Highway 64 onto Old Highway 64 for 0.2 mile, then turn west onto State Route 1310, also called Wayah Bald Road. Arrowwood Glade Picnic Area, along the creek, has a covered shelter, flush toilets, drinking water, and horseshoe pits to help you stretch out after riding in the car.

The byway climbs west through the dense forest alongside Wayah Creek. Wayah is Cherokee for "wolf," which were eliminated from this area long ago. Black bears remain, however, and the forest is a designated sanctuary for them.

Beautiful mountain streams and rivers often border Mountain Waters Scenic Byways.

The Appalachian National Scenic Trail intersects the scenic byway at Wayah Gap. You can hike 4.5-miles of this 2,132-mile trail: the section leading to the summit of Wayah Bald. Or drive there on Forest Road 69. Views from the top of the handsome stone tower include the surrounding Nantahala Mountains, the Cowee Mountains, and the town of Franklin. Also in this vicinity is the first station on the Nantahala National Forest, Wilson Lick Ranger Station, built about 1913.

The spring blossoming of flame azaleas and white azaleas along Wayah Bald Road are renowned throughout the region. Bring your camera. But don't overlook the slightly less showy wildflowers: violets, bluets, butterfly weeds, Indian paintbrushes, trilliums, and fleabanes. Due in part to the climate, the area's plant species are some of the most diverse in the world.

Continuing on the scenic byway brings you alongside Nantahala Lake, a 29-mile reservoir, dammed in 1942 to create electricity. The power station 5.5 miles downriver generates 23,700 kilowatt-hours each year for the western part of the state. With accessible boat ramps (one right on the byway) boating on the reservoir is excellent, and anglers fish for trout, bass, and other cold-water fish. You'll find several country stores and other services scattered along the lake.

Dropping down to the Nantahala River (good trout fishing), stop at Camp Branch Falls for yet another view of a splendid waterfall. A little farther along, whitewater boaters launch trips down this well-known section of wild water. You'll find numerous river outfitters willing to take you down the river.

The byway intersects U.S. Highway 19 and travels north on it. You've just entered the splendid Nantahala River Gorge. "Nantahala" is a Cherokee word meaning "land of the noon day sun." With its steep, tall side slopes rising vertically from the river, the only time the sun shines in the gorge is around noon. The river is one of the most popular whitewater rivers in eastern North America, with an 8.5-mile stretch that can be kayaked, canoed, boated, or rafted. Water enthusiasts make their way through the gorge where they'll see mixed hardwoods and pines growing between the rock outcroppings.

Pull over for a ringside seat to watch the whitewater boaters negotiating Patton's Run. You're likely to see more than a few thrilling moments as they maneuver through the rapids.

A few miles farther through the river gorge, Ferebee Memorial Recreation Area has picnic tables and grills, and a boat launch. It's quite amusing to "eavesdrop" on the excited chatter of boaters who are taking out after running the rapids. If you love to watch it or want to relive your own trip, stop again at Nantahala Falls to watch more whitewater boaters running the rapids.

The Great Smoky Mountains Railway runs through the gorge, providing perfect views of the river and boaters, the dramatic gorge, and abundant, lush vegetation. It's a perfect way to relax and take in lots of sights without the driver having to miss a lot because the road demands so much attention. The train runs from Bryson City to the Nantahala Gorge.

Day hikers and through hikers cross the gorge on another segment of the Appalachian Trail at Wesser. Another popular trail that crisscrosses the byway is the Bartram Trail, named after famous naturalist William Bartram. It heads into the gorge paralleling the Nantahala Bike Trail, a 2-mile paved trail that starts on State Route 1310 and is also very popular for walking and jogging.

Mountain Waters Scenic Byway ends at the intersection of U.S. Highway 19 and U.S. Highway 28. The opportunities for beautiful scenery and recreation, however, continue in every direction.

26

Forest Heritage Scenic Byway
Pisgah National Forest

General description: A 79-mile loop through forest and countryside.

Special attractions: Cradle of Forestry in America, Pisgah State Fish Hatchery, Looking Glass Rock Scenic Area, Looking Glass Falls, Sliding Rock, Shining Rock and Middle Prong wilderness areas, hiking and nature trails, exceptional trout fishing, abundant wildlife, spring blossoms.

Location: Western North Carolina on the Pisgah National Forest and in Haywood and Transylvania counties, south of Asheville. The byway is a loop that travels from Brevard northwest on U.S. Highway 276, south on North Carolina Route 215, and northeast back to Brevard on U.S. Highway 64.

Byway route numbers: U.S. Highway 276, North Carolina Route 215, U.S. Highway 64.

Travel season: Year-round. Occasional snow and ice may require use of chains in winter.

Camping: Five national forest campgrounds, two for individual camping, three for groups. All have drinking water, picnic tables, fire grates, and toilets. Some with showers and trailer dumping station. Suitable for tents, truck campers, and trailers less than 16 feet in length. No hookups. Campgrounds generally open from April through November.

Services: All services in Brevard and in nearby communities of Balsam Grove, Canton, Rosman, and Waynesville.

Nearby attractions: Blue Ridge Parkway, Folk Art Center and Biltmore House in Asheville, Brevard Music Center, Carl Sandburg Home National Historic Site, Flat Rock State Theater near Hendersonville.

For more information: See the appendix for contact information.

The Drive

North Carolina's first scenic byway provides a sampling of some of the state's best mountain scenery. The route passes through dense forests of conifers and hardwoods, along bold mountain trout streams, through picturesque farmlands, and across high mountain ridges. Part of the route follows old settlement roads and logging railroads that were developed in the late 1800s and early 1900s.

Drive 26: Forest Heritage Scenic Byway

Pisgah National Forest

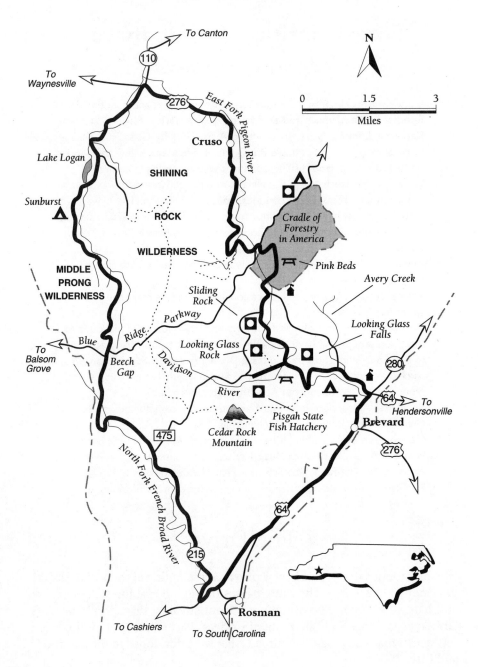

Much of the forest in this area was heavily logged in the early 1900s, but recovery has been so complete that today the forest looks nearly untouched. It is composed primarily of oaks, yellow poplars, and birches. Forest inhabitants include deer, black bears, gray squirrels, groundhogs, wild turkeys, gray foxes, and opossums.

Elevations range from a low of 2,230 feet at Brevard to more than 5,340 feet where the byway crosses the Blue Ridge Parkway at Beech Gap.

Western North Carolina has four distinct seasons. Summers and winters are moderate. Even the hottest months seldom reach the 90s. But watch for sudden and severe thunderstorms during late summer. Foliage is at its most colorful around the second and third weeks of October, sometimes lasting until early November. The area has occasional snow and ice during the winter, but winter storms are usually short-lived.

The Pisgah District is one of the most popular areas in the state, and traffic can be heavy, particularly in summer and during the fall color season. The paved highways are steep and winding with frequent sharp curves. Pisgah is the biblical name of the mountain from which Moses saw the promised land, and a local pastor probably introduced the name here in the late 1700s.

Anglers can choose from several excellent trout streams. The upper section of the Davidson River was rated by *Trout* magazine as one of the 100 best streams in America. Limited to fly fishing, the stream is renowned for its hefty populations of brown and rainbow trout. The lower section below Avery Creek has brown, brook, and rainbow trout. The East Fork of the Pigeon River, a native brook-trout stream, also offers excellent fishing.

The only large developed area on the byway is the city of Brevard, county seat of Transylvania County. Established in 1861, the city is the home of Brevard College and the Brevard Music Center, one of the nation's leading summer music camps. The music center offers more than 50 musical programs and public concerts from mid-June to mid-August, with everything from classical music and pops concerts to operas and Broadway musicals.

Although there are several access points, the official beginning of the scenic byway is on U.S. Highway 276 near Brevard, a few hundred feet beyond the stone columns that mark the entrance to Pisgah National Forest. An exhibit contains a map that highlights points of interest along the route. Brochures, maps, and information about area attractions are available about 1 mile farther up U.S. Highway 276 at the ranger station-visitor center. A side road just beyond the visitor center leads to English Chapel, a Methodist church founded in 1869 and still used by area residents and visitors. It is the only remaining structure of a small community that used to be in the area.

Sycamore Flats is a large picnic area on the banks of the Davidson River. You can wade in the river and enjoy the shade of the numerous sycamore trees that grow along the bank.

Sliding Rock gives visitors a wet thrill along the Forest Heritage Scenic Byway.
Robert B. Satterwhite photo

Davidson River Campground, with 161 forested or grassy sites, is the largest and busiest camping area along the byway. Davidson has hot showers and a trailer dumping station.

About 5 miles west of the starting point, a side trip on Forest Road 475 follows the Davidson River away from U.S. Highway 276 and leads to the Pisgah State Fish Hatchery, open daily for tours. The state Wildlife Resources Commission operates the hatchery and raises thousands of rainbow, brook, and brown trout from eggs. When the trout are between seven and nine inches long, they are released in general trout waters throughout the western part of the state.

Several hiking trails are accessible from Forest Road 475. Your best bet is the 3.1-mile trail that leads to the summit of Looking Glass Rock, a granite monolith that glistens with seeping groundwater. In winter, the water freezes on the rock's smooth face and reflects the sun like a mirror, or looking glass. Views from the top of the rock are spectacular and include Cedar Rock, the Blue Ridge Parkway, and the Pink Beds.

Peregrine falcons were reintroduced to this area, and in summer they nest and raise their young on the rock cliffs of Looking Glass Rock. You may also see an occasional golden eagle soaring overhead.

Just beyond the fish hatchery road is Looking Glass Falls—one of the most scenic and best-known falls in the eastern United States. Water tumbles over a massive overhanging shelf about 30 feet wide into a deep pool 60 feet below. You can park and walk to the bottom of the falls via stairs.

At Sliding Rock, the next stop on the byway, a sheet of water cascades over a 60-foot-long, gently sloping, slick-as-glass rock, creating a natural water slide. Watch from an observation deck, or don cutoffs and a T-shirt and join the hundreds of others on the slide. It's hard to resist. Be prepared for a breathtaking plunge into the icy pool at the bottom of the falls. The water is cold even during the hottest months. The slide is open for a fee, from Memorial Day through Labor Day. There is a bathhouse, and lifeguards are on duty from 10 A.M. to 5:30 P.M. daily.

The Cradle of Forestry in America is a National Historic Site that commemorates the birthplace of scientific forestry and forestry education in the United States. This area, located just beyond Sliding Rock, has a visitor center, exhibits, interpretive film show, gift shop, snack bar, and two walking trails. The Biltmore Forest School Campus Trail is a 1-mile paved path that goes by the restored and reconstructed buildings used by the first forestry students at the turn of the century. The Forest Festival Trail, also paved and 1 mile long, features early 1900s forestry exhibits, including a 1915 Climax logging locomotive and steam-powered sawmill. The Cradle of Forestry is open May through October from 9 A.M. to 5 P.M. A nominal entrance fee is charged. New exhibits include the giant tree, mountain stream and dynamic forest, and a firefighting helicopter simulation.

The last major point of interest on U.S. Highway 276 is the Pink Beds Picnic Area. This mountain valley is covered with thick growths of native rhododendrons, mountain laurels, and flame azaleas. Blooming season runs from spring to summer, with peak bloom time in June. Visitors come from miles around to marvel at the splendid display of floral blossoms.

The byway continues northwest on U.S. Highway 276 and intersects the Blue Ridge Parkway. Below the parkway, the route crosses the East Fork of the Pigeon River, where a trailhead offers three footpaths into the Shining Rock Wilderness. The byway leaves the national forest and descends along the East Fork of the Pigeon River to Cruso, a small mountain community in Haywood County. According to local legend, the community's first postmaster, who had just read *Robinson Crusoe*, named the area.

A few miles beyond Cruso, the Forest Heritage Scenic Byway loops south on North Carolina Route 215, still following the river. Lake Logan was created in 1932 to supply water to the paper mill. It is privately owned. A few miles farther, Sunburst Campground is located right on the river. Sunburst has drinking water, picnicking, hiking, and fishing.

Past Sunburst, the byway passes between the Middle Prong and Shining Rock wilderness areas, which were logged in the 1920s. Major forest fires in 1925 and 1942 burned extensive acreage. Today the region is covered with small trees and rhododendrons.

The highway climbs past several pretty waterfalls along the West Fork of the Pigeon River to Beech Gap, elevation 5,340 feet. Here the byway again passes under the Blue Ridge Parkway. Views along this section are spectacular, but the road is winding and has few pullouts.

Beyond Beech Gap, the road follows the North Fork of the French Broad River through mountain pastures and forest. Several area trout farms supply fish to restaurants. South of the Blue Ridge Parkway, Alligator Rock juts over the byway, and North Carolina Route 215 ends at its junction with U.S. Highway 64. Travel north on U.S. Highway 64 through the countryside to Brevard. The byway passes through the middle of town, past the courthouse and Brevard College campus. Traveling just a few miles north completes the scenic byway loop.

—Robert B. Satterwhite

27

Oscar Wiggington Memorial Scenic Byway

Sumter National Forest

General description: A 14-mile highway through the wooded foothills of the Blue Ridge Mountains.

Special attractions: Excellent trout fishing, National Wild and Scenic Chattooga River, hunting, trout hatchery, Ellicott Rock Wilderness, scenic waterfalls, hiking trails, Oconee State Park.

Location: Northwest corner of South Carolina on the Sumter National Forest, east of Greenville. The byway begins at the Oconee State Park and runs north to the South Carolina-North Carolina state line.

Byway route number: South Carolina Route 107 and South Carolina Route 413.

Travel season: Year-round. Occasional temporary closure for ice, generally in January or February.

Camping: One national forest campground with 29 sites, picnic tables, fire grates, and flush toilets. One state park with 140 sites and hookups. Additional national forest campgrounds nearby.

Services: Groceries and gift shop in Oconee State Park. All services in nearby Walhalla, Seneca, and Clemson, and in Cashiers, North Carolina.

Nearby attractions: Lakes Jocassee, Keowee, and Hartwell; Clemson University; Whitewater Falls; Cherokee Foothills Scenic Highway; abandoned railroad tunnel.

For more information: See the appendix for contact information.

 The Drive

Located in the extreme northwest corner of South Carolina in the gentle foothills of the Blue Ridge Mountains, the Oscar Wiggington Scenic Byway is known as the gateway to the mountains. The paved, easy-to-drive two-lane road ascends from 1,778 feet to 2,900 feet, and it has frequent scenic turnouts and recreational opportunities.

This area is cooler and wetter on a year-round basis than the adjoining Piedmont section of South Carolina. From December through March, low temperatures average in the 20s and highs in the 50s. April, May, and October

Drive 27: Oscar Wiggington Memorial Scenic Byway
Sumter National Forest

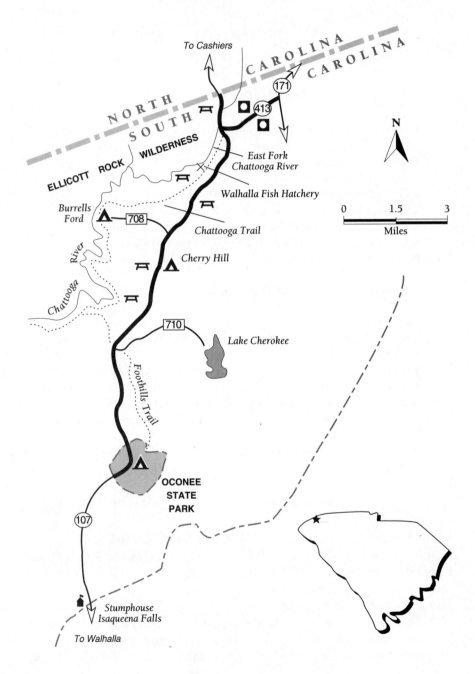

have temperatures in the 40s through 70s, and June through September average in the 60s to 90s. Expect rain about 90 days of the year, with January, February, March, and July the wettest months.

In the early days, Cherokee warriors came through the area on their way to conquer the Piedmont tribes. The high plateaus and mountains were the last strongholds of the Cherokees in South Carolina before they moved out in 1792, after signing a peace treaty.

The Sumter National Forest boundary is north of Walhalla on South Carolina Route 28. At the boundary, you will find the Stumphouse Ranger Station, which has visitor information, and the Stumphouse Tunnel and Park. You can walk 1,600 feet into the pre-Civil War, never-completed railroad tunnel as it winds into the solid granite mountain. It was abandoned in the 1850s due to lack of money. Clemson University, South Carolina's famous agricultural college, used the tunnel at one time to cure the renowned Clemson Bleu Cheese. Walls of the curing room are still visible. The tunnel and adjacent park are on the National Register of Historic Places.

Near the tunnel is Issaqueena Falls, rich in Indian legend, and a pleasant 5-mile hiking trail along an abandoned railroad bed.

Two miles north of the ranger station, turn north onto South Carolina Route 107. Two more miles lead to Oconee State Park and the beginning of the scenic byway. Oconee State Park is one of the gems of the South Carolina state park system. Tucked away in wooded areas that border a crystal-clear, 20-acre lake fed by two cool mountain streams are family rental cabins and a 140-site campground. All campsites have water and electrical hookups. There are modern restrooms with hot showers. A store at the entrance to the camping area has groceries, film, souvenirs, and camping supplies. Square dancing, clogging, nature trails, and programs by park naturalists highlight park activities.

The forests are composed predominantly of white and loblolly pines, hickories, and red and white oaks. During the autumn, the byway is crowded with visitors who come to view the vivid foliage colors. Peak viewing is around mid-October. Spring visitors are attracted to the showy display of flowering mountain laurels, dogwoods, and rosebay and catawba rhododendrons.

Birdwatchers enjoy spotting red-tailed, sharp-shinned, and Cooper's hawks, American kestrels, bluebirds, mockingbirds, Carolina wrens, wood thrushes, and cardinals. Wildflowers include trilliums, sunflowers, asters, butterfly weeds, and fawn's breath.

A side trip on Tamassee Road follows an old trail used by the Cherokees to get to Lake Cherokee. This is also one of the points where the Foothills Trail crosses South Carolina Route 107. This 85-mile hiking trail rambles across the upper part of South Carolina and links Oconee State Park with

Visitors are welcome to view the operations at Walhalla National Forest Fish Hatchery, along South Carolina State Highway 107. LARRY CRIBB PHOTO

Table Rock State Park via Whitewater Falls. It crosses some of the most rugged, beautiful terrain in the Carolinas.

Cherry Hill Campground has 22 sites in the trees and a bathhouse, drinking water, fishing and hiking opportunities, picnic tables, fire grates, and a trailer dumping station.

A half mile farther is Moody Springs Recreation Area. In addition to the picnic grounds and toilet facilities, there is a spring that some local people believe has medicinal properties.

A side trip on Burrells Ford Road leads 3 miles to a shallow portion of the Chattooga River, where a wagon road crossed the river. The powerful Chattooga, which has been designated a National Wild and Scenic River, descends almost 2,500 feet in its 50-mile length. The river is the western boundary of the Sumter National Forest and the state line between South Carolina and Georgia. There is excellent fishing for brown and rainbow trout, challenging boating and rafting, and beautiful hiking trails along the banks. Floating is permitted on a 28-mile stretch of the river. Information on canoe rentals and guided trips is available at the ranger station.

Part of the Appalachian Chain, the Blue Ridge Mountains were formed some 320 million years ago when the continental plate that contained Africa collided with the continental plate that contained North America. The collision thrust a section of the earth's crust skyward to form mountains that were as high and majestic as today's Himalayas. For the past 200 million years, these plates have been pulling apart and the Appalachian Mountains gradually wearing away. This pulling apart has also formed the Atlantic Ocean. There are igneous and metamorphic rocks here, such as mica schist and granitic gneiss.

Burrell's Place is a roadside picnic area, and 1 mile farther is the entrance to the Walhalla State Fish Hatchery and the Chattooga Picnic Area. The winding 2-mile road down the side of the mountain features exciting hairpin turns and an excellent look at the forest. Near the parking lot, a footbridge leads over the East Fork of the Chattooga to the fish hatchery, where you can see brood stock of rainbow and brown trout. The hatchery raises millions of trout fingerlings annually, and the U.S. Fish and Wildlife Service stocks streams in South Carolina, North Carolina, and Georgia with these fish.

Another path out of the hatchery parking lot leads into Ellicott Rock Wilderness, which contains giant old-growth eastern hemlocks and white pines. Some tower more than 200 feet high. Rhododendrons and mountain laurels abound, and the forest feels much like a rain forest. On a summer day, it can be 15 to 20 degrees cooler here than in the surrounding territory.

This trail gives the opportunity to journey 0.25-mile into real wilderness. The Ellicott Rock Wilderness was named for a surveyor hired to locate the disputed border for South Carolina, North Carolina, and Georgia. In 1811, he chiseled his mark in a rock at the survey's ending point on the South Carolina bank of the river. The trail runs right along the beautiful stream that is the East Fork of the Chattooga River.

A breathtaking view is available at the Wiggington Cutoff, North Carolina Route 413. Two overlooks about 0.25-mile off the byway are high above Lake Jocassee. About 3 miles farther down the side road, you reach pretty Whitewater Falls.

Sloan Bridge Recreation Area is the last picnic area on the byway before the South Carolina-North Carolina state line. South Carolina Route 107 travels through a beautiful mountain landscape and offers a look at the mountain culture of the lower Appalachian Mountains.

—*Larry Cribb*

28

Ridge and Valley Scenic Byway

Chattahoochee National Forest

General description: A 47-mile loop drive along scenic ridges and through lush valleys.

Special attractions: Johns Mountain, wildflowers, autumn colors, hunting, picnicking, camping.

Location: Northwest Georgia on the Chattahoochee National Forest. The byway travels an oblong loop out of Villanow, east on Georgia State Highway 136, south on Furnace Creek Road, Pocket Road, Johns Creek Road, and Floyd Springs Road, southwest on Georgia State Highway 156, northwest on U.S. Highway 27, and back north on Thomas Ballenger Road and East Armuchee Road.

Byway route numbers: Georgia State Highway 136, Furnace Creek Road, Pocket Road, Johns Creek Road, Floyd Springs Road, Georgia State Highway 156, U.S. Highway 27, Thomas Ballenger Road, East Armuchee Road.

Travel season: Year-round.

Camping: One national forest campground, with picnic tables, fire grates, toilets, drinking water.

Services: Traveler services in Villanow, as well as in nearby Summerville, LaFayette, Dalton, Calhoun, Ringold, and Rome.

Nearby attractions: Chickamauga and Chattanooga National Military Park, Cloudland Canyon and James H. "Sloppy" Floyd state parks, Chattanooga urban activities.

For more information: See the appendix for contact information.

 The Drive

Ridge and Valley Scenic Byway traverses an eye-catching region of long, narrow ridges and wide, fertile valleys. The two-lane roads are paved; some have narrow shoulders and some provide numerous scenic turnouts. Traffic on U.S. Highway 27 is constant; the other roads are moderately busy.

Summer days are hot and somewhat humid, with temperatures in the 70s to low 90s. Nights are cooler, in the 50s to 70s. Spring and fall temperatures generally range from the 50s to the 70s. Expect some snow in winter, with daytime temperatures in the 40s and 50s and nights dropping to freezing.

The byway is very scenic driven in either direction. Beginning in

Drive 28: Ridge and Valley Scenic Byway

Chattahoochee National Forest

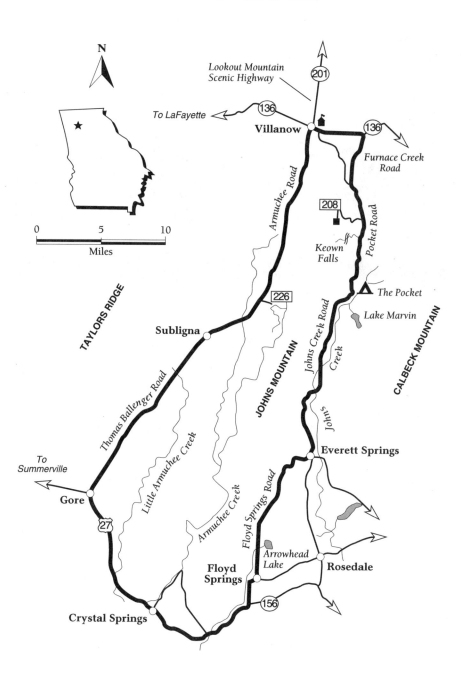

Lake Marvin offers a serene place to relax along the Ridge and Valley Scenic Byway.
CHATTAHOOCHEE NATIONAL FOREST PHOTO

Villanow and driving in a clockwise direction, go east on Georgia State Highway 136, then follow Furnace Creek Road and Pocket Road south through the forest. A side trip west on Forest Road 208 leads to a good overlook on Johns Mountain. You can see Georgia, Alabama, and Tennessee from this 1,800 foot elevation.

The ridge and valley physiographic region of the Appalachian Mountain Range is easy to see here. Long, narrow ridges have a characteristic southwest to northeast trend, and between the rocky ridges lie fertile valley bottoms with farms and creeks.

The turnoff to Keown Falls Scenic Area is west on Forest Road 702. This 218-acre recreation area has picnic tables, and a 1.8-mile loop trail through the forest to an observation deck overlooking a set of two waterfalls. It's an easy walk and a good opportunity to stroll through a lovely region.

The forest is primarily southern hardwoods such as white, northern red, and black oaks, yellow poplars, beech, sourwood, and shagbark hickory. Some shortleaf and Virginia pines are found along the highway. Azaleas and dogwoods usually bloom in April, and late October is the best time to view the brilliant colors of autumn leaves.

Johns Mountain has a variety of wildlife, including white-tailed deer, turkeys, racoons, skunks, chipmunks, gray squirrels, and fox squirrels. Look overhead to see soaring red-tailed hawks.

Continuing south on the byway, The Pocket Recreation Area has 27 campsites along a pretty little spring-fed stream that runs between the steep ridges of Horn Mountain. An easy 2.5-mile loop trail winds through the woods and offers a pleasant way to enjoy the area.

The byway follows Johns Creek, a fast-flowing, rocky stream stocked with rainbow trout. The road winds through the dense forest, with steep mountainsides on both sides. At Everett Springs, turn west and follow Floyd Springs Road south through a rural setting. There are hayfields, cattle, farms, and residences in the valley. Johns Mountain rises to the west; Calbeck Mountain is to the east. There are a few picnic tables at Arrowhead Lake, and you can fish for bass, bluegill, and catfish.

The byway leaves the mountains in Floyd Springs and travels southwest on Georgia State Highway 156, then northwest on U.S. Highway 27 to Gore. You'll then drive north on Thomas Ballenger Road, paralleling Taylors Ridge on the west. Old barns are picturesque, and the pastoral valley is quite pretty.

At Subligna, bear northeast on Armuchee Road. A side trip east on Forest Road 226 leads to dispersed, primitive campsites and good redeye bass fishing in Armuchee Creek. Back on the byway heading north, you'll get some of the best views of Taylors Ridge and Johns Mountain. "Armuchee" is an Indian word meaning "land of wildflowers." Wildflowers you may see along the byway include pink lady's slipper, goldenrod, Queen Anne's lace, daisies, Solomon's seal, gaylax, trillium, and fire pinks.

The byway completes the loop in Villanow. The quaint general store there has been operated continuously since 1847.

29

Russell-Brasstown Scenic Byway

Chattahoochee National Forest

General description: A 38-mile loop alongside streams and waterfalls and through forested hills with a side trip to the top of Brasstown Bald, the highest mountain in Georgia, and then down again.

Special attractions: Colorful autumn foliage, outstanding views, a scenic Bavarian-style town, Brasstown Wilderness, Raven Cliff Wilderness, Mark Trail Wilderness, mountain streams, waterfalls.

Location: North Georgia on the Chattahoochee National Forest, northwest of Toccoa. The byway is a loop that follows Georgia Route 17/75 from Helen north to an intersection with Georgia Route 180 near High Shoals, turns west on Georgia Route 180 to its intersection with Georgia Route 348, goes south on Georgia Route 348, then goes northeast to Georgia Route 356. Follow Georgia Route 356 to Georgia Route 17/75.

Byway route numbers: Georgia Route 17/75, Georgia Route 180, Georgia Route 348, and Georgia Route 356.

Travel season: Year-round, with occasional temporary closures for winter snow removal.

Camping: One national forest campground with drinking water, toilets, picnic tables, and fire grates. No hookups. Two nearby state parks with more than 180 sites, hiking trails, picnic tables, fire grates, toilets, drinking water, hookups, and a trailer dumping station.

Services: All services in Helen and in nearby Blairsville, Cleveland, and Hiawassee.

Nearby attractions: Anna Ruby Falls, Hiawassee drama and country shows, Lake Chatuge, Lake Winfield Scott, Track Rock Gap, Unicoi and Vogel state parks.

For more information: See the appendix for contact information.

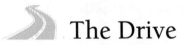 The Drive

Showcasing some of the most spectacular and diverse scenery in Georgia, the popular, paved Russell-Brasstown loop lies entirely within the Chattahoochee National Forest.

Expect temperatures ranging from as high as 95 degrees in summer to as low as zero in winter. The weather on Brasstown Bald and the peaks

Drive 29: Russell-Brasstown Scenic Byway
Chattahoochee National Forest

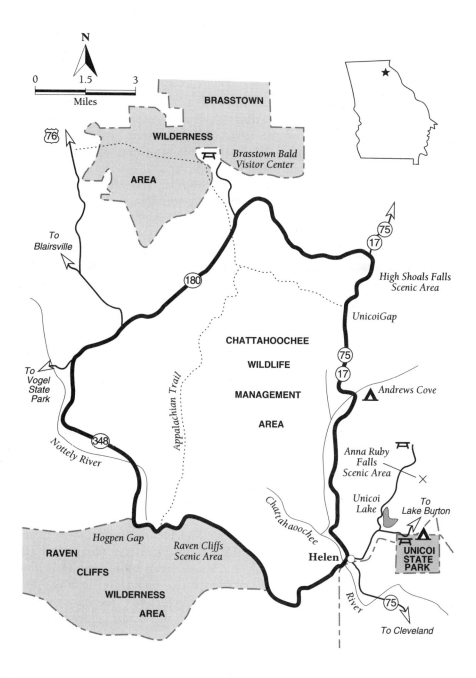

along Richard Russell Scenic Highway (Georgia Route 348) is more severe; the highest recorded temperature was 84 degrees and the lowest a frigid minus 27 degrees.

The scenery is exceptional throughout the route. Travel along the Richard Russell Highway portion is fairly light except in autumn, when colorful leaves draw spectators in droves. Other portions of the roadway are regularly traveled highways. Elevations vary from 1,600 feet to Brasstown Bald's 4,784 feet.

The route begins at fairy-tale-like Helen, a cocoon-to-butterfly story of ingenuity on the part of its citizenry. Once a sleepy sawmill town, it underwent a transformation in the 1960s. Buildings were given a Bavarian look, and tourism increased in this pretty mountain community.

The headwaters of the Chattahoochee River, which flows south to the Gulf of Mexico, are located near Helen. The river, generally crystal-clear, provides top-notch trout fishing downtown. A trout festival is one of several annual Helen events.

Unicoi State Park is 3 miles north of Helen via Georgia Route 17/75 and Georgia Route 356. This is a delightful side trip from the scenic byway. The park has 80 campsites. Just above the park, in the Chattahoochee National Forest, you can reach Anna Ruby Falls via an easy, paved 0.5-mile footpath from the visitor center. An observation deck offers a striking view of the twin falls of York and Curtis creeks. A 1,600-acre scenic area surrounds it.

Driving north along winding Georgia Route 17/75, you will see beautiful views of forested hills and mountains. Andrews Cove, 5 miles north of Helen along Andrews Creek, has camping, fishing, and hiking. Five miles farther north, out-of-the-way High Shoals Scenic Area has a 1-mile hike past five waterfalls.

Fauna of the Chattahoochee National Forest includes white-tailed deer, black bears, wild turkeys, opossums, grouse, squirrels, foxes, groundhogs, and raccoons. Flora includes rhododendrons, mountain laurels, flame azaleas, dogwoods, serviceberries, sourwoods, and many species of wildflowers. Tree species range from sturdy pines, poplars, and hemlocks to majestic oaks.

Less than 0.5 mile north of the High Shoals turnoff, the byway turns west onto Georgia Route 180. Six miles away is the intersection of Georgia Route 180 and Georgia 180 spur, a 2.5-mile steep route leading to the Brasstown Bald fee parking lot. The interpretive bookstore there is open seven days a week from Memorial Day through October. You have the option of either hiking the steep trail 0.5 mile to the visitor center atop the mountain or paying a small fee to take a shuttle. The visitor center has a video program and interpretive exhibits that tell about the area, as well as

Mountain music entertains visitors at the gift shop in the Brasstown Bald parking lot.
DAN COOK PHOTO

an observation deck with a view of four states.

Short day-hiking opportunities include two trails that leave from the parking lot: the 4.5-mile Jack Knob Trail leads to the Appalachian Trail at Chattahoochee Gap, and the 5.5-mile Arkaquah Trail goes west to Track Rock Road. Both trails are moderately difficult.

The name Brasstown Bald is derived from a misunderstanding of the Cherokee Indian word "itséye." It means "new green place" or "place of fresh green." It applied particularly to a tract of ground made green by fresh vegetation after having been cleared of timber. Early settlers thought the Cherokee were saying "untsaiyi'" which means "brass place."

Geologists believe this section of the Blue Ridge Mountains is more than 300 million years old. On the north side of Brasstown Bald are communities with a distinct geologic substrate—fields of angular rock or blocks of rock with little visible subsoil. The large, angular boulders were split by the action of glaciers in the Pleistocene age. The areas, mostly north facing, may date back at least 10,000 years.

A number of "balds," a description for treeless mountaintops of the area, stirred Indian thoughts. According to legend, a terrible monster disturbed the peaceful Cherokee nation long ago. It carried away the children of the villages, and the Indians were unable to capture or kill the beast. They cleared the mountaintops of all timber in order to observe the flight of the beast. Later the den of the marauder was located in the cliffs of a mountain. Two braves ascended the tallest hemlocks and were horrified to observe the brood of young beasts to which the monster has been feeding the children. The Indians then sought the aid of the Great Spirit, who sent down a bolt of lightning to destroy the monster and its brood. The Indians offered thanks to the Great Spirit and in turn received a promise that never again would the mountaintops be covered with timber.

Returning from Brasstown to Georgia Route 180, the route west provides some lovely pastoral views for 8 miles before connecting with the Richard Russell Scenic Highway (Georgia Route 348). The first 4 miles travel south through farm county on the headwaters of the Nottely River. After reaching the national forest boundary, the byway proceeds up the mountains to Hogpen Gap, which is the Blue Ridge Divide separating the water draining into the Tennessee River on the west and the Chattahoochee on the east. Stop at the overlook on the north side of the road just before the top for a view of the visitor center atop Brasstown Bald. The drainage just below is called Lordamercy Cove for its steep and rugged landscape.

The Appalachian Trail, a 2,100-mile footpath from Georgia to Maine, crosses the byway at Hogpen Gap. It also crosses the byway between Helen and Hiawassee at Unicoi Gap.

From here the remaining segment of the scenic byway follows Georgia Route 348 east toward Helen. The national forest land on the south side of the highway is part of the Raven Cliff Wilderness. To the north is part of the Mark Trail Wilderness. Several fine day hikes are available. Raven Cliff Trail goes 2.5 miles into the wilderness area to Raven Cliff Falls; the hike is moderately difficult. The Dukes Creek Falls Trail winds 0.8 mile from the parking lot into Dukes Creek Gorge to the falls. This trail is steep.

Complete the byway loop by turning left on Georgia Route 356 and following it to Georgia Route 17/75.

—Dan Cook

30

Apalachee Savannahs Scenic Byway

Apalachicola National Forest

General description: A 31-mile paved highway through pine forest, riverine systems, and savannahs.

Special attractions: Camping, hunting, fishing, abundant wildlife, wildflowers, unusual plants, Fort Gadsden Historic Site.

Location: Northwest Florida on the Apalachicola National Forest, south of Chattahoochee. The byway follows County Road 12 from the national forest boundary south of Bristol south to its intersection with County Road 379, then County Road 379 south to Sumatra, and south again on Florida Route 65. The byway ends just north of Buck Siding at the national forest boundary.

Byway route numbers: County Road 12 and County Road 379, Florida Route 65.

Travel season: Year-round.

Camping: Three national forest campgrounds with water, picnic tables, fire grates, and flush toilets. No hookups.

Services: All services in Bristol, Blountstown, Apalachicola, Eastpoint, and Carrabelle.

Nearby attractions: Torreya State Park, historic Gregory Home, Apalachicola River, Mud Swamp-New River Wilderness, Bradwell Bay Wilderness, Florida National Scenic Trail, Ochlockonee River, Lake Talquin.

For more information: See the appendix for contact information.

The Drive

Set in the pine forests and savannahs of the Florida panhandle, the Apalachee Savannahs Scenic Byway runs roughly parallel to the imposing and historic Apalachicola River. The two-lane highway is paved, and there are frequent access roads of graded dirt or clay that are sequentially numbered. Traffic is light and the highway is well-maintained. The landscape is composed of southern yellow pine forests, savannahs, cypress stands, and abundant wildflowers in season, such as milkworts, bachelor buttons, grass pinks, coreopsis, blazing stars, and black-eyed Susans.

Summer visitors should be prepared for temperatures in the 90s and 100s, high humidity, and frequent rain. Spring and fall are more moderate,

Drive 30: Apalachee Savannahs Scenic Byway
Apalachicola National Forest

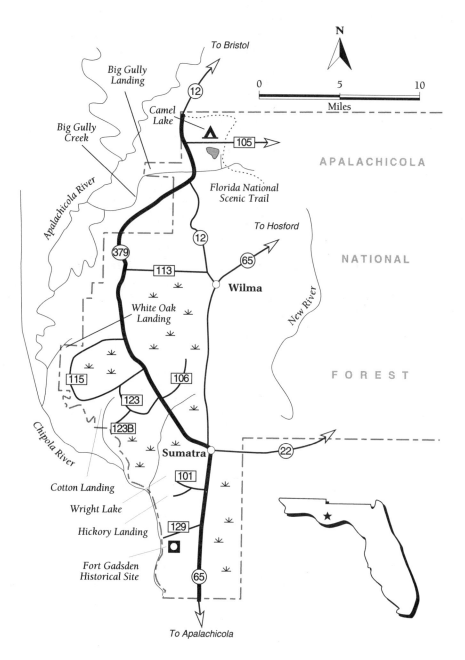

and winter travelers may encounter lows in the 30s and 40s in January and February.

Bristol is a small, rural community near the Apalachicola River. The scenic byway begins 7 miles south of Bristol on County Road 12, at the national forest boundary. One mile south of the boundary, Camel Lake Recreation Area offers excellent camping opportunities on the banks of a small scenic lake surrounded by cypresses, oaks, and pines. There are ten campsites, a swimming area, a boat ramp, picnic tables, and public restrooms. Fishing for bass and bream is good, and dove hunting is permitted in season.

Farther south on the byway, the thick pine forest is interspersed with bay and cypress swamps. The forest provides habitat for many wildlife species, including black bears, deer, wild turkeys, squirrels, bobcats, alligators, foxes, opossums, and gopher tortoises. The latter burrow in the ground, creating underground refuges for many other species. The red-cockaded woodpecker, an endangered species, prefers to nest in mature longleaf pines. Showy orchids and lilies, as well as carnivorous insect-eating pitcher plants and bladderworts, grow in the boggy treeless areas called savannahs.

An unusual activity practiced in the forest is a rural technique of worm gathering called grunting. A wooden stake is driven into moist soil and rubbed across the top with a heavy piece of iron. This transmits underground vibrations that drive worms to the surface. The technique provides anglers with plenty of worms for bait.

After crossing Big Gully Creek, drive less than 1 mile to the intersection of County Road 12 and County Road 379. The byway continues south on County Road 379. A side trip west on Forest Road 133 leads to Big Gully Landing, the first in a series of public boat launches. Fishing is good for bass, bream, and catfish in Big Gully Creek, which also provides access to the Apalachicola River.

Continuing south on County Road 379, you pass a quaint, deserted church and cemetery, as well as vast expanses of broom sedge and a few miles of private, agricultural land. The tilled fields offer a marked contrast to the tall stands of timber that line the road within the national forest.

The byway has frequent access roads that branch to the east and west. County Road 379A leads west 2 miles to a fee boat launch into the Florida River, part of a system of creeks and rivers that feed into the giant Apalachicola River. Just south of County Road 379A is Forest Road 115, which goes to White Oak Landing on the River Styx. The 3-mile drive on Forest Road 115 travels past a series of rather quaint campers and trailers, offering a rare view of life in rural Florida off the beaten path. The route skirts the north end of Big Cypress Swamp. Huge cypress stumps rise from the boggy area near the road, where an interpretive sign indicates a "Hydric Hardwood Swamp."

The Apalachee Savannahs Scenic Byway provides many access points to the Apalachicola River and other waterways of the Florida panhandle. WILLIAM A. GREER PHOTO

Farther south on County Road 379, the vista opens up. Large savannahs, maintained treeless by prescribed fires, are bordered by pine stands on the east and west. Forest Road 123 leads west 4 miles through thick palmetto underbrush full of birds and wildlife. The landscape is subtle, and fresh green ferns cover the forest floor in burned areas. The route ends at Cotton Landing, which has four campsites, picnicking, and toilets available. Fishing and canoeing are fun in Kennedy Creek.

The next side trip is Forest Road 106. This graded road offers particularly good opportunities for viewing a wide variety of wildflowers and insectivorous plants. Here pitcher plants, Venus flytraps, sundews, bladderworts, and orchids grow in abundance and can be photographed with ease.

The byway offers dramatic views of stands of dwarf cypresses near the highway. Three miles south of Forest Road 106, the tiny town of Sumatra has a one-room post office, a church, several residences, and one convenience store with a restroom and phone. The byway then follows Florida Route 65 south.

South of Sumatra, a side trip west on Forest Road 101 leads to Wright Lake and Hickory Landing recreation areas. Hickory Landing has ten campsites set in a mixed pine and hardwood forest close to the stream bank. The boat launch accesses Owl Creek, where you can fish for bass and bream. Wright Lake has 25 sites in the tall pines adjacent to the lake. Swimming, canoeing, and fishing are fun in the crystal-clear waters of Wright Lake.

The last side trip leads west on Forest Road 129 to Fort Gadsden Historic Site. Interpretive exhibits depict the history of Fort Gadsden and the part it played in Florida's history. The fort was particularly important because of its strategic location on the Apalachicola River, a major transportation route during the Civil War. Today contours in the ground indicate the location of the fort on a bluff overlooking the river. There is a covered picnic area, a restroom, and a small outdoor museum with artifact displays and a lighted diorama of the fort. Literature about the fort is available at the site.

The entire area is underlain by limestone bedrock, probably from the Miocene age. Native Americans have inhabited this area along the Apalachicola River for 10,000 to 12,000 years. Arrowheads and pottery shards found in fields and along river and creek banks must be left there, to preserve our heritage.

The byway ends just north of Buck Siding, a mere bend in the road at the national forest boundary. Motorists continuing south and west will pass through the fishing town of Eastpoint, and then Apalachicola, a town well worth a stop. It has some fine Victorian architecture and the John Gorrie Museum. The recently restored Gibson Hotel, dating from the 1880s, is in the center of town and offers food and repose with an excellent view of Apalachicola Bay.

—*William A. Greer*

31

Talladega Scenic Drive

Talladega National Forest

General description: A 23-mile highway along the crest of Horseblock Mountain into Cheaha State Park.

Special attractions: Extensive vistas, Cheaha Wilderness, Lake Chinnabee Recreation Area, Pinhoti Trail, Cheaha State Park, Cheaha Park, autumn foliage, hiking, camping, fishing.

Location: East-central Alabama on the Talladega National Forest. The byway travels Alabama State Highway 281 from its junction with U.S. Highway 78 3 miles west of Heflin, south through Cheaha State Park to Turnipseed Hunter Camp, just outside the state park.

Byway route number: Alabama State Highway 281.

Travel season: Year-round.

Camping: Four state park campgrounds. Two provide only drinking water, and are within walking distance of bathhouse facilities. Two campgrounds are fully developed, with power, sewer, and water hookups, fire grates, picnic tables, bathhouses.

Services: Food, lodging, and small store in Cheaha State Park. All traveler services in nearby Anniston, Oxford, Talladega, Munford, and Heflin.

Nearby attractions: Pine Glen and Coleman Lake recreation areas, Clay County Public Lake, DeSoto Caverns.

For more information: See the appendix for contact information.

 The Drive

The Talladega Scenic Drive takes you up a long ridge with a splendid, far-ranging view, to popular Cheaha State Park. The two-lane highway is paved and has frequent turnouts. Traffic is moderately light, but increases during the fall color season, between about late October until the end of November.

Summer daytime temperatures average in the mid 80s to the low 90s, and humidity is very high. Expect frequent late afternoon thundershowers. Summer nights may cool to the 60s. Spring and fall temperatures range from the mid 60s to 70s, dropping to 40 or 50 at night. Winter days in February and March are usually in the 40s and 50s but may drop to the high 30s, with a rare freeze. Most rain falls in winter and spring.

The route is pleasant driven in either direction. When traveling north-

Drive 31: Talladega Scenic Drive
Talladega National Forest

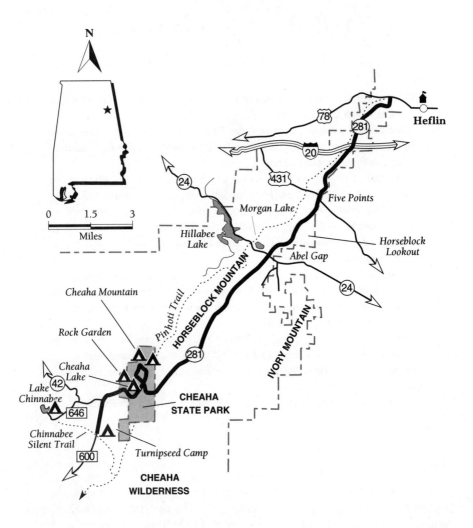

east to southwest, the scenic byway begins 3 miles west of Heflin on U.S. Highway 78 and follows Alabama State Highway 281 southwest along a ridge overlooking wooded valleys and farmland communities. Numerous scenic overlooks allow a leisurely view of the surrounding area, including Cheaha Mountain, Dugger Mountain, and Horseblock Lookout.

While driving the byway, you'll pass numerous access points to the Pinhoti Trail. The Pinhoti Trail is a popular horseback and backpack trail, stretching over 80 miles across the Talladega National Forest and Cheaha State Park.

The byway crosses over the interstate, winds through Five Points, and climbs on both sides and provides extensive views in both directions. You can look west to the Coosa River Valley and the town of Oxford. The national forest dominates the foreground.

You could hike up the old road to the base of Horseblock Lookout, for another view of the area. One mile or so farther north, take a side trip west to Morgan Lake on graveled County Road 24. There you can picnic, fish for smallmouth bass and crappie, and take a walk along the lake on a portion of the Pinhoti Trail. East on County Road 24 takes you to Abel Gap's pretty little white church that looks especially picturesque at sunrise.

The Talladega Scenic Drive continues along Horseblock Mountain, with views of Ivory Mountain to the east. In the 1940s, prospectors found some gold in Ivory Mountain's streams. Just north of the county line, a jeep road runs northwest. You could walk a few miles on it to see the hand-laid rockwork done by the Civilian Conservation Corps (CCC) in the 1930s. There are stone culverts and reinforcing walls, and the stone bridge over Hillabee Creek is quite beautiful.

The byway now enters Cheaha State Park, which charges a small fee for day use. Cheaha is taken from the Choctaw Indian word "chaha," which means high. There are abundant recreation opportunities in the park. Take a side trip north to the top of Cheaha Mountain, the highest point in Alabama at 2,407 feet. The view is splendid, and on a clear day you may see sixty miles. The surrounding tree-covered mountains are beautiful, and you can see the towns of Anniston to the north, and Talladega to the west.

The primary tree species are shortleaf pine, mixed with hardwoods such as red oak and hickory. Wild azalea blossoms provide a stunning display each spring, and rival summer foliage for beauty.

This area is the southern end of the Appalachian Mountain Range, a northeast to southwest trending series of parallel ridges. The dominant rock types are granite and quartz. You'll see lots of scenic white-colored quartz rock outcrops and cliff faces in the park.

The CCC who worked here in the 1920s and 1930s built the summit observation tower. The CCC also built the cabins, bathhouses, and dam. At

The Talladega Scenic Drive winds through Alabama.

the top of Cheaha Mountain there is a restaurant, store, motel, group lodge, two campgrounds, a picnic area, and various short walking paths. The summit is a popular place for rappelling, hang-gliding, and cliff-climbing.

Wildflowers throughout the park include goldenrod, rosinweed, pokeberry, blazing star, wild indigo, horseweed, golden aster, bluebell, and flowering spurge.

Wildlife watchers can look for white-tailed deer, red fox, and wild turkeys, as well as skunks, racoons, squirrels, and possums. The rare red-cockaded woodpecker inhabits the surrounding Talladega National Forest.

Another good viewpoint in the park is from the Rock Garden, a scenic rock outcrop. A very short footpath leads to a view of the sheer cliffs, and Cheaha Lake below.

You may see turkey vultures or red-tailed hawks soaring overhead. Other birds in the park include cardinals, wrens, and finches. You'll likely see lots of eastern bluebirds, too. The park has an active bluebird recovery program, and there are lots of nesting boxes throughout the park.

Stretch your legs on the Odom Scout Trail, which begins in the park on Alabama State Highway 281. You can make a day of the whole 11-mile trail, or walk out a few miles and return. There are lots of lookout points as you wind through the trees along the top of the ridge.

The road drops about 1,200 vertical feet from the top of Cheaha

Mountain to Cheaha Lake. At the lake you'll find two more campgrounds, one primitive and one developed, as well as a swim beach, and good fishing possibilities for bluegill, catfish, and bass.

The scenic byway leaves the state park and reenters the Talladega National Forest. The route is very pretty, rambling along ridges and through the forest, with occasional views out to the west.

A side trip west on Forest Road 646 brings you to Lake Chinnabee Recreation Area. The lake is picturesque, situated in a little mountain valley. The campground has 13 sites right on the lakeshore. Anglers cast for bass and bream and hikers have several good trails to walk. The Lakeshore Trail encircles the lake in an easy 2-mile hike. Chinnabee Silent Trail is moderately strenuous, and follows Cheaha Creek about 3 miles from the lake up to Forest Road 600. The views along the trail are very nice.

Just east of the byway, the Cheaha Wilderness protects 7,490 acres of rugged terrain. The forest on the lower slopes is composed of white, scarlet, and chestnut oaks, hickories, and longleaf and shortleaf pines. On the higher ridges chestnut oak and Virginia pine are dominant.

The byway ends near Turnipseed Camp, a historic hunting camp. The campground provides drinking water and toilets. The road continues on as Forest Road 600. This gravel route is best suited for high-clearance vehicles.

32

Natchez Trace Scenic Byway

Tombigbee National Forest

General description: A 17-mile Y-shaped route along a landscaped parkway, to a pretty lake.

Special attractions: Davis Lake, Indian Mounds, Owl Creek, historic features, camping, hunting, and fishing.

Location: Northeast Mississippi on the Tombigbee National Forest. The byways travel the Natchez Trace Parkway between the national forest boundaries east of Houston and south of Tupelo. The spur on Chickasaw County Road 903 leads between the parkway and David Lake.

Byway route number: Natchez Trace Parkway and Chickasaw County Road 903.

Travel season: Year-round.

Camping: One national forest campground at Davis Lake, with picnic tables, fire grates, showers, toilets, RV hookups, trailer dump station, and drinking water.

Services: No traveler services on the byway. All services in Houston and nearby Tupelo.

Nearby attractions: Tupelo National Battlefield, Trace State Park, Brices Cross Roads National Battlefield Site, Tupelo State Park, Chickasaw Village.

For more information: See the appendix for contact information.

 The Drive

Natchez Trace Scenic Byway travels a Y-shaped route along a portion of the Natchez Trace Parkway, with a spur road west to Davis Lake. The two-lane roads are paved. The parkway has wide shoulders and frequent scenic turnouts and is a popular bicycle route. Traffic is generally light to moderate. The spur road to Davis Lake is narrow, and traffic moves slowly.

Summers are long and hot, with frequent heavy thunderstorms. Daytime highs can reach 100 degrees with 60 to 70 percent humidity. Nights don't offer much relief. Spring and fall are more pleasant, with temperatures ranging from the 60s to the 80s. Winter temperatures can drop to the teens at times.

The byway is very scenic driven in either direction. Driving on the

Drive 32: Natchez Trace Scenic Byway
Tombigbee National Forest

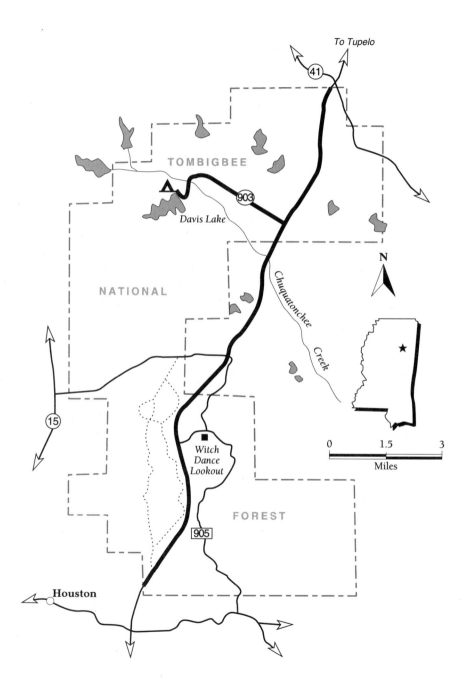

Natchez Trace Parkway from north to south, the byway begins at the national forest boundary and winds through a closed canopy of trees. Tree species include loblolly pines; southern and northern red oaks; white oaks; shagbark, mockernut, and pignut hickories; Eastern redcedars; shortleaf pines; dogwoods; red maples; and sweet gums. The state tree is the southern magnolia, commonly found in the wetter, streamside areas along the byway.

Spring and autumn tours are spectacular. Dogwoods and redbud provide a beautiful display of spring blossoms, usually beginning in early April. About the middle of October, the hardwoods begin turning brilliant reds, golds, and yellows.

Wildflower enthusiasts will find plenty of blossoms. Look for agave, jack-in-the-pulpit, golden club, spiderwort, iris, star grass, wild hyacinth, fairy wand, and fawn lily, among others.

This region was once under a great inland salt sea. In places you can still see a white chalky soil from the limestone and eroded and weathered seashells. Stop at a roadside exhibit to see fossils of marine organisms.

Hunting is a popular activity on the national forest. Hunters look for white-tailed deer, turkeys, quail, squirrels, and ducks.

The byway turns west on a spur road and travels through rural farms and pastures toward Davis Lake. The Owl Creek Indian Mounds are listed on the National Register of Historic Places. This is a series of five mounds built around a central plaza. Two of the mounds were built by Native Americans sometime between 1000 and 1300 A.D., and used for religious ceremonies. It is very interesting to stop here.

Two-hundred-acre Davis Lake provides multiple recreation opportunities. There is a fine grassy swimming beach and good fishing for largemouth bass, hybrid striped bass, crappie, catfish, and bream. The campground has 24 sites on the lake. You can pull your boat right up to many of the campsites. A 2-mile fishing trail wanders along the north edge of the lake to several earthen fishing piers.

Bird watchers can look for Canada geese, snow geese, and a variety of ducks including mallards, pintails, canvasbacks, wood ducks, and black ducks. Songbirds and raptors are plentiful and include meadowlarks, tanagers, bluebirds, chickadees, and thrashers. Look overhead for soaring red-tailed and sparrow hawks, and watch herons fish along stream banks. The distinctive "coo" of mourning doves is a pretty sound. You may spot a shy fox or even a bobcat in the forest.

Return to the parkway and turn south again. The landscape varies from timberlands to farmlands. Primary crops in this region are soybeans, cotton, and corn. Stop for a hike along Witch Dance Horse Trail, a 9- or 15-mile riding trail. You can hike this loop through the forest. Note the vegetation

*A beautiful forest of southern hardwoods and pines surrounds the
Natchez Trace Scenic Byway.* TOMBIGBEE NATIONAL FOREST PHOTO

changes from the higher lands at the beginning of the loop, to the lower
bottomlands. Witch Dance is named for an old superstition claiming that
when witches met here to dance, the grass died each place their feet touched
the ground.

The byway continues south on the parkway and ends at the national
forest boundary near Houston.

33

Longleaf Trail Scenic Byway

Kisatchie National Forest

General description: A 17-mile paved highway offering lovely views of the pine uplands of the Kisatchie Hills.

Special attractions: Rugged terrain and fast-flowing streams, warm-water fishing, Kisatchie Hills Wilderness, National Red Dirt Wildlife Management Preserve, hiking trails, logging and pioneer history.

Location: Central Louisiana on the Kisatchie National Forest, south of Natchitoches. The byway follows Forest Road 59 on national forest lands between Louisiana Route 119 and Louisiana Route 117.

Byway route number: Forest Road 59.

Travel season: Year-round.

Camping: Seven national forest campgrounds. Some have drinking water, tables, and vault toilets. Best suited to tents or truck campers, but some sites can accommodate larger motor homes. No hookups.

Services: All services in Natchitoches. Gas, groceries, and phones at several nearby communities, including Derry, Kisatchie, Rosepine, Gorum, and Provencal.

Nearby attractions: Natchitoches, the oldest settlement in the Louisiana Purchase, historic Fort St. Jean Baptiste, several antebellum homes predating the Civil War and statehood.

For more information: See the appendix for contact information.

 ## The Drive

The Longleaf Trail Scenic Byway winds along a ridge top through the unique Kisatchie Hills and features outstanding views of rocky outcrops, distant hills and buttes, and Kisatchie Bayou's sparkling water and white sand beaches. Elevation ranges from 80 feet in the creek bottoms to 400 feet in the hills. Visible from some distance, the hills are flanked by countryside that ranges from pastoral pecan orchards and cotton fields to heavily forested bayous and hill country. The Kisatchie Hills are a real jewel in the heart of Louisiana.

The two-lane road is paved and has numerous scenic turnouts at overlooks and interpretive areas. Gravel side roads lead to campgrounds and other areas of interest.

Fine stonework and picturesque settings enhance the many scenic overlooks along the Longleaf Trail Scenic Byway. JIM CALDWELL PHOTO

The central Louisiana climate is characterized by hot, humid summers with intense, local thunderstorms. July and August are the hottest months, with average temperatures of about 82 degrees. Winters are short and mild; the temperature averages about 47 degrees in December and January. Winter rains often last several days. The frost-free season usually extends from the end of March to the beginning of November.

The picturesque city of Natchitoches boasts waterfront architecture reminiscent of that in New Orleans. The old main street looks out on Cane River, a placid oxbow lake abandoned long ago by the meandering Red River. Northwestern State University, agriculture, and the wood-products industry are important factors in Natchitoches' commerce. Tourism has increased in recent years, primarily because of the area's rich history and unique scenery.

Driving Longleaf Trail from east to west, the byway sweeps gently up from flat, bottomland agricultural country in to the pine uplands. The route then parallels the southern boundary of the Kisatchie Hills Wilderness for about 7 miles. The Civilian Conservation Corps (CCC) constructed the Longleaf Trail as a single-lane road in about 1935.

The Kisatchie Hills area is composed of two ancient sandstone beds that stand higher than the sandstone in the surrounding area. The area is known as the Kisatchie Wold, part of a unique line of upland hills that cross central Louisiana from Toledo Bend Reservoir on the Sabine River to Sicily Island, near the Mississippi River.

Drive 33: Longleaf Trail Scenic Byway

Kisatchie National Forest

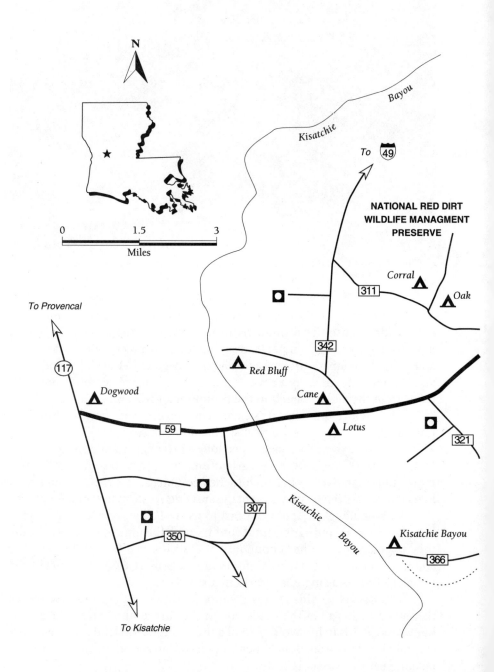

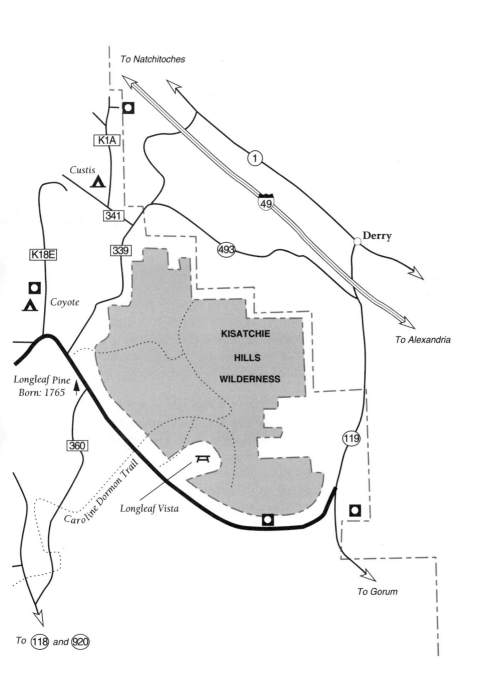

To Natchitoches

K1A

Custis

341

K18E

339

Coyote

Longleaf Pine
Born: 1765

360

Caroline Dormon Trail

Longleaf Vista

To 118 and 920

1

49

493

Derry

KISATCHIE

HILLS

WILDERNESS

To Alexandria

119

To Gorum

The wold is composed of silica-cemented sandstone, a result of the weathering of volcanic ash. It is highly resistant to erosion, and as the surrounding countryside wore down and the Gulf of Mexico sank, the wold remained prominently high. Petrified wood and opals are found in this area.

Just west of Bayou Cypre Overlook, for about 2 miles, the byway follows the original Opelousas-to-Fort Jesup Military Road, an important route used during the Civil War.

Longleaf Vista has picnic tables, restrooms, and drinking water, as well as the 1.5-mile Longleaf Vista Nature Trail. The trail passes near the remains of a late nineteenth- and early twentieth-century turpentine still, and it also provides access to the old narrow-gauge rail bed used for hauling timber and naval supplies. The vista point offers a sweeping panorama of Kisatchie Hills Wilderness and its unspoiled forest setting. This rugged 8,700-acre wilderness is known locally as the "Little Grand Canyon," and it has popular hiking trails. The Backbone Hiking and Equestrian Trail is a moderately difficult 12-mile path into the wilderness area. It follows ridge lines, allowing wonderful views of the sandstone bluffs and rock formations unique to the Kisatchie Hills area.

Kisatchie Ranger District lies within the traditional range of late prehistoric Caddo Indians. Several unmarked sites occupied during that time are within 1 mile of the byway.

About 1 mile west of Longleaf Vista, the 12.5-mile Caroline Dormon Hiking and Horse Trail extends to Kisatchie Bayou Campground. It is named in memory of the woman credited with pushing through legislation that resulted in the creation of Kisatchie National Forest, the only national forest in Louisiana.

Early loggers would occasionally leave a fine tree, possibly as a seed source. The Statesman Tree, just beyond the Caroline Dormon Trailhead, is about 175 years old—very old for a southern pine. It is typical of the trees that covered the Kisatchie Hills in the centuries before logging.

Forest Road 360 and Forest Road 321 lead to Kisatchie Bayou Campground. This scenic area is located on the bluffs overlooking white sand beaches, rocky rapids, and sandy bottomlands of mixed hardwoods and pine. You can camp, picnic, fish, canoe, and hike. There are vault toilets and drinking water available. Anglers fish for Kentucky striped bass, sunfish, and catfish.

Loblolly and longleaf pines dominate the forest, with mixed hardwoods such as hickories, dogwoods, and black, post, southern red, and white oaks in the drainages and along ridge tops. Blossoming dogwoods and wild azaleas brighten spring.

Farther west along the byway, Forest Road 339, Forest Road 341, and Forest Road K1A make a nice side trip through the forest to Custis Campground, which is inside the 38,450-acre National Red Dirt Wildlife Management Preserve. This is a popular hunting camp, but it has no facilities. A bit north of the campground, on Forest Road K1A, is Melrose Overlook, from which you can see eastward over fields and farms. Roadside wildflowers include asters and coreopsis.

About midway along the byway, you will find Coyote Campground and Overlook, Oak Campground, and Corral Campground. These areas are popular with hunters from October 1 until April 30, and they have no developed facilities.

As turn-of-the-century loggers moved through the virgin forests of the Kisatchie Hills, they sometimes left small or deformed trees. One of these trees, about 238 years old (is west of Forest Road 360), is a reminder of past consumptive logging operations. Many are infected with red heart disease, a decay common to mature southern pines. Trees such as these are favorite nesting and roosting places for the endangered red-cockaded woodpecker, the only woodpecker known to build nests in cavities within living trees. Nest trees are banded with white paint for easy identification on Forest Road 321.

Other forest inhabitants include white-tailed deer, foxes, squirrels, raccoons, opossums, coyotes, quail, songbirds, and occasional roadrunners.

Forest Road 321 passes by a red-cockaded woodpecker colony and provides another access to Kisatchie Bayou Campground. Red Bluff Campground and Eagle Overlook are found off Forest Road 342. Red Bluff is located on the lower stretches of Kisatchie Bayou, where the bayou is deeper and less sandy than in other areas. Flush toilets are provided.

Across from Cane Campground, Lotus Campground, which has drinking water and vault toilets, is situated in a pretty upland hardwood forest. An old well is all that remains of the Lotus School site, the first school in the area. A historic stagecoach route from southern Louisiana intersects the byway near here.

Kisatchie Bayou crosses Longleaf Trail just east of Forest Road 307. The bayou is included in the Louisiana Natural and Scenic Stream system. Local Indians referred to it as Kisatchie, meaning "Cane Country," because of the switch cane patches that grow along the stream. Kisatchie Bayou is unique among the characteristically quiet bayous of Louisiana. It has a steep enough stream gradient that its rapids and falls greet you with exciting sights and sounds that you normally would expect to find only in the mountains of the eastern or western United States.

At its western end, Longleaf Trail Scenic Byway intersects with Louisiana Route 117. Near this junction, more than 100 years ago, Bellwood Academy was located on the present site of the Kisatchie Work Center. The academy offered advanced studies in several fields, but it closed in 1863. Also nearby is Dogwood Campground, set among the pines, hardwoods, and, of course, dogwood trees. This campground has drinking water, restrooms, and an interpretive display.

—Ron Couch

34

St. Francis Scenic Byway

St. Francis National Forest

General description: A 20-mile paved and gravel route along the top of Crowleys Ridge, offering extensive views of forests and Mississippi River delta.

Special attractions: Far-ranging views, Bear Creek Lake, Storm Creek Lake, boating, fishing, regional festivals.

Location: East-central Arkansas on the St. Francis National Forest, near the border with Mississippi. The route follows Arkansas Route 44 from the national forest boundary near Marianna, south to Forest Road 1900, and continues south on Forest Road 1900 to its terminus at the national forest boundary near West Helena.

Byway route numbers: Arkansas Route 44 and Forest Road 1900.

Travel season: Year-round.

Camping: Four national forest campgrounds with picnic tables, drinking water, toilets, fire grates, and boat-launch facilities. No hookups.

Services: No services on the byway. All services in Marianna, Helena, and West Helena.

Nearby attractions: St. Francis, L'Anguille, and Mississippi rivers, White River National Wildlife Refuge, agricultural museum in Stuttgart, regional festivals and celebrations, Memphis music festivals, King Biscuit Blues Festival in Helena.

For more information: See the appendix for contact information.

 The Drive

The St. Francis Scenic Byway winds atop a unique ridge in eastern Arkansas through a beautiful hardwood forest. The 20-mile route is paved for about 9 miles and is well-maintained with graded gravel the remaining miles. Traffic is constant in the summer and light the rest of the year.

Summers are humid and hot, with temperatures ranging from 70 to 100 degrees. Spring and autumn temperatures range from 50 to 80 degrees, and winters average in the 40s to 60s. Most precipitation falls between March and May.

Driving north to south, the route begins near Marianna, where a ranger station has national forest and byway information. The city also has a small

Drive 34: St. Francis Scenic Byway
St. Francis National Forest

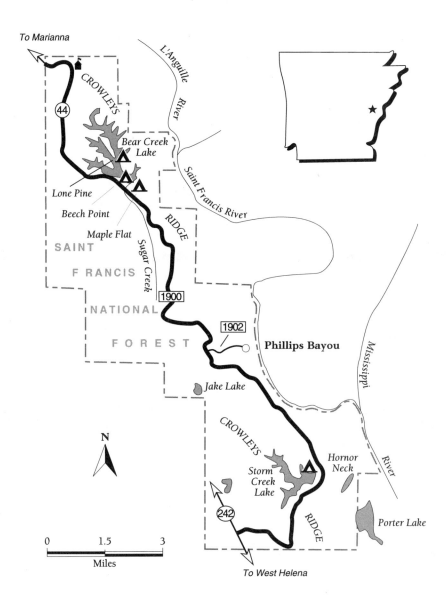

museum, and the Chamber of Commerce is housed in a restored historic building.

The byway crosses 5 miles of rolling terrain south to Bear Creek Lake. The 625-acre lake is rated as one of the best fishing lakes in Arkansas. Fish species include bass, crappie, catfish, and bream.

Bear Creek Lake has two campgrounds and an overflow group campground, for a total of 46 sites. The peaceful campgrounds are situated in the trees and fields near the shore. Swimming, picnicking, fishing, and boating are popular recreational activities at Bear Lake. Bring mosquito repellent. A 0.5-mile loop trail in the lakeshore area was completed in 1992.

The byway continues south atop the ridge on Forest Road 1900. The surrounding forest is one of the largest hardwood stands in eastern Arkansas. The soils on the ridge are very fertile, and the trees grow large. Foliage colors in autumn are spectacular. The forest includes white and red oaks, hickories, sumacs, yellow poplars, American beeches, cypresses, swamp black gums (locally called tupelos), and American sycamores. The lush understory includes papaws, ironwoods, hydrangeas, spicebushes, dogwoods, redbuds, ferns, and Carolina magnolia vines. In spring the flowering shrubs are lovely, with blossoms hovering like a cloud of mist in the forest.

About midway through the scenic byway, Forest Road 1902 leads east to the small community of Phillips Bayou on the St. Francis River. There are boat launches and fishing opportunities on the river here.

Forest inhabitants include white-tailed deer, wild turkeys, rabbits, raccoons, armadillos, skunks, opossums, and a variety of squirrels. Bird watchers will see many species. Waterfowl such as colorful wood ducks and great blue herons are on the lakes, and songbirds include bluebirds, orioles, cardinals, jays, and wrens. Crowleys Ridge is on the Mississippi Flyway, and spring and fall bring the unmistakable sound of thousands of honking geese flying overhead.

The byway route runs atop Crowleys Ridge, a unique geological formation. The north-south ridge is about 200 miles long and 4 to 9 miles wide. The ridge has a thick accumulation of windblown soil, or loess. Surrounding lands below the ridge are typical river-bottom deltas—flat, productive farmlands. For many decades, early farmers along the ridge burned off the thick vegetation, and the fine soils eroded into steep gullies and slopes. In 1932 the Soil Conservation Service acquired the ridge and let hardwood trees reclaim the badly damaged land. Today the ridge supports a thriving and productive hardwood forest. Most of the harvested timber goes to the furniture and flooring industries.

Continuing south on Forest Road 1900, you will reach Storm Creek Lake, which covers 420 acres. The lake features popular swim and picnic areas, as well as a fishing pier. Anglers fish for striped bass, crappie, catfish,

The St. Francis Scenic Byway brings motorists to 625-acre Bear Creek Lake, considered one of the best fishing lakes in Arkansas. St. Francis National Forest photo

and bream. The campground has 12 sites near the lakeshore. At the northwest end of the lake, a Research Natural Area hosts a 400-acre forest of hundred-year-old trees. One yellow poplar has a trunk three feet in diameter. The area somehow escaped human interference during the early settlement years, and today national forest managers have a policy of no management so that researchers and students may study the largely untouched area.

The byway follows Forest Road 1900 south to its terminus at Arkansas Route 242, near West Helena. In nearby Helena, the Delta Cultural-Historical Center located in a historic train station is open for public tours.

35

Sylamore Scenic Byway

Ozark National Forest

General description: A 26.5-mile drive through the hardwood forests of the rolling Ozark Mountains to Blanchard Springs Caverns.

Special attractions: Blanchard Springs Caverns and Information Center, colorful autumn foliage, White River.

Location: North-central Arkansas on the Ozark National Forest, northwest of Batesville. The route follows Arkansas Route 5 from Calico Rock south to Allison and Arkansas Route 14 from Allison west to Blanchard Springs Caverns.

Byway route numbers: Arkansas Route 5 and Arkansas Route 14.

Travel season: Year-round.

Camping: One national forest campground with picnic tables, showers, drinking water, fire grates, and trailer dumping station. Two additional national forest campgrounds nearby.

Services: All services in Calico Rock, and nearby Mountain View.

Nearby attractions: Ozark Folk Center, regional festivals and celebrations, Leatherwood and Lower Buffalo wilderness areas, Buffalo National River.

For more information: See the appendix for contact information.

 The Drive

The Sylamore Scenic Byway is a J-shaped route that parallels the White River atop its plunging white limestone cliffs, climbs a high ridge, and winds along the top to Blanchard Springs Caverns. The two-lane highway is paved and has turnouts for scenic and recreational opportunities. Traffic is moderate from June through October and very light the rest of the year. The Arkansas Folk Festival at Mountain View kicks off the tourist season the third weekend in April.

Spring and autumn temperatures are generally very pleasant, with daytime temperatures in the 50s and 60s. Summers are humid, and there are frequent afternoon thunderstorms. Daytime temperatures are usually in the 80s and 90s. Winter days are usually above freezing and may get up to the 60s. Nights drop below freezing, and ice or sleet is common in January and February.

Drive 35: Sylamore Scenic Byway

Ozark National Forest

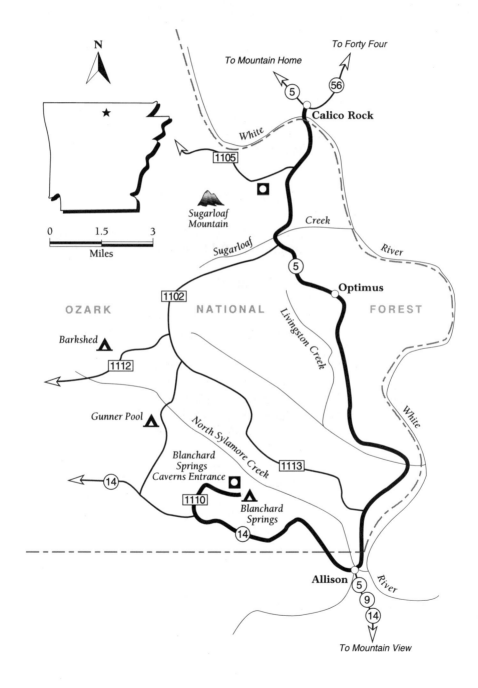

The byway can be entered at Allison via Arkansas Route 9. Driving from north to south, begin in Calico Rock, a rural community on the White River. This broad, meandering river is floatable year-round. Anglers will enjoy fishing for brown and rainbow trout.

The byway passes fenced pastures and agricultural lands near the White River. The area is part of the northern Arkansas limestone belt, deposited by ancient seas 460 million years ago. The oval-shaped Ozark Dome was uplifted, and breaks and fractures developed to relieve the internal pressures. Limestone, sandstone, shale, and chert were exposed by the fractures and by subsequent stream erosion.

The byway crosses Sugarloaf Creek and continues south through Optimus to follow Livingston Creek. The hills are primarily blanketed in white oaks, hickories, and stands of shortleaf pines. The USDA Forest Service manages the byway area as a scenic corridor. Numerous fields host sassafras, blackberry bushes, and flowering plums.

Ozark National Forest inhabitants include white-tailed deer, wild turkeys, squirrels, rabbits, opossums, skunks, black bears, and raccoons. Bird watchers can look for more than 150 species of birds, including cardinals, robins, blue jays, warblers, and finches. Bald eagles are occasionally seen in winter. Endangered Indiana and gray bats inhabit caves on the national forest. About 250,000 gray bats winter in one cave on the district; they represent about a sixth of the known population of that species. Ticks and chiggers can be annoying in spring and summer, and walkers should watch for poison ivy and oak and stinging nettle, as well as occasional poisonous snakes.

The byway continues south across rolling hills, offering pretty views of the forest and fields. The White River flows below, contained within high limestone cliffs. The route turns west at Allison, onto Arkansas Route 14.

A 6-mile side trip through Allison to Mountain View brings you to this charming Ozark community that emphasizes folk arts. The Ozark Folk Center State Park has more than 24 activities and interpretations that recreate the turn-of-the-century mountain lifestyle. Live music and jigs, clogging, and waltzes brighten the dance floor, and the arts and traditional crafts flourish. There is lodging and a restaurant at the state park, and Mountain View offers all services to travelers.

Back at Allison, turn west onto Arkansas Route 14. The road climbs to Government Hill, which provides far-reaching views of the Ozark Mountains. The winding route runs atop the ridge to Blanchard Springs Caverns Recreation Area, the end of the byway.

Blanchard Springs offers a variety of activities, including hiking, camping, swimming, fishing, nature programs, cavern tours, and picnicking. You could easily spend a few days here.

Springtime blossoms along the Sylamore Scenic Byway include dogwoods and redbuds.
OZARK NATIONAL FOREST PHOTO

The campground has 32 sites along North Sylamore Creek. The creek has some great swimming holes, and it is fun to tube. Anglers fish for small-mouth bass in the creek and rainbow trout in Mirror Lake. During the summer Forest Service naturalists lead evening programs about the many interesting features of the Ozark National Forest, their topics ranging from natural history to local folk culture. The programs are held in the Shelter Cave Amphitheater, at the base of a big sandstone bluff.

Blanchard Springs Caverns has a visitor center and guided tours. Information and exhibits explain the caverns, and a movie provides a good introduction to the area.

The limestone caverns are still growing and changing. You can choose to walk the 0.4-mile Dripstone Trail through the upper levels of the caverns, which is easy walking, or you can follow the more strenuous 1.2-miles Discovery Trail through a stream-carved corridor. Speleothems, or cave formations, include giant columns, travertine dams, fragile soda-straw stalactites, and gleaming crystalline flowstones. Minerals color the formations in shades of orange, brown, yellow, blue, black, and gray. Unusual insects and animals have adapted to the unique environment. They include the endangered gray bat and the colorless Ozark blind salamander.

This area offers plenty of hiking opportunities. Sylamore Creek Hiking Trail follows the creek 15 miles, beginning near Allison and passing through Blanchard Campground to reach Barkshed Picnic Area to the northwest. There are several access points, and you can hike anywhere from 1.5 to the full 15 miles. The hiking trail is linear and has no loops. The footpath sometimes meanders close to the creek and other times climbs the adjacent limestone bluffs. Hikers may see a shy deer or startle a lizard sunning on the rocks.

There is a new 0.5-mile disabled-accessible trail at the Visitor Center, as well as a 1.5-mile trail to Blanchard Springs. Disabled visitors can also go down the wooden trail to fish from the new pier at Mirror Lake.

36

Ozark Highlands Scenic Byway

Ozark National Forest

General description: A 35-mile route traversing the upper ridges and highlands of the Boston Range in the Ozark Mountains.

Special attractions: Colorful autumn foliage, spring blossoms, extensive views, abundant wildlife, Upper Buffalo Wilderness, hunting, Ozark Highland Trail.

Location: West-central Arkansas on the 1.1-million-acre Ozark National Forest, east of Fort Smith and north of Interstate 40. The byway follows Arkansas Route 21 on national forest land between Boxley and Clarksville.

Byway route number: Arkansas Route 21.

Travel season: Year-round.

Camping: One national forest campground with picnic tables, drinking water, fire grates, and toilets. No hookups.

Services: Ozone, Fallsville, and Edwards Junction have gas and groceries. All services in nearby Clarksville, Boxley, and Jasper.

Nearby attractions: Buffalo National River; Dardanelle Reservoir; Eureka Springs; Silver Dollar City in Branson, Missouri; War Eagle Craft Fair; Peach Festival in Clarksville; Dogpatch USA; and Mount Magazine, Arkansas Highway 7, Pig Trail, and Sylamore national forest scenic byways.

For more information: See the appendix for contact information.

 The Drive

The Ozark Highlands Scenic Byway travels some of the highest elevations of the Ozarks, and panoramic views are extensive. The two-lane highway is paved and has pullouts for scenic and recreational access. This is a major highway, and traffic is light to moderately heavy.

Summer temperatures range from the 60s through the 90s, and humidity is moderate. Spring and autumn are cooler, with temperatures in the 40s to 80s, while winter temperatures drop below freezing at night and climb to the 40s or 50s by day.

Driving from north to south, begin near the Buffalo National River, a popular recreation area with floating, swimming, fishing, hiking, and camping opportunities.

Drive 36: Ozark Highlands Scenic Byway
Ozark National Forest

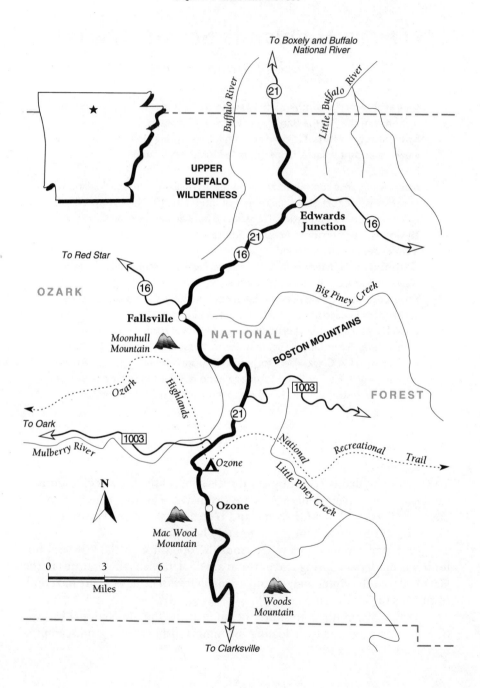

Backpackers enjoy a winter trek along the 140-mile-long Ozark Highlands National Recreation Trail, accessible from the Ozark Highlands Scenic Byway. Tim Ernst photo

The byway runs just east of the Upper Buffalo Wilderness, which protects the headwaters of the Buffalo River from human intervention and pollution. The wilderness encompasses 12,035 acres of hardwood forest with scenic sandstone and limestone outcrops and mountainous terrain.

The byway goes south through Edwards Junction, where Arkansas Route 16 joins Arkansas Route 21 for 8.5 miles. The byway runs atop high ridges, paralleling Moonhull Mountain and the headwaters of the Mulberry River, which has premier canoeing farther down, beginning in Oark. This upper section is very scenic and offers seasonal fishing.

The forest vegetation is thick, with several species of oaks and hickories and scattered stands of native shortleaf pines represented. The understory is rich with springtime blossoms of redbuds, dogwoods, serviceberries, wild plums, and vacciniums, or berry bushes. In autumn the sumacs, sassafras, and Virginia creepers add bright colors to the forest foliage.

Forest inhabitants include white-tailed deer, black bears, and wild turkeys, as well as abundant songbirds such as indigo buntings, cardinals, blue jays, and finches. There are red-tailed hawks, crows, and barred owls, and in winter bald and golden eagles are occasionally sighted along the river or soaring over the ridges.

Ozone Campground is situated in the tall pines and has eight sites. The 165-mile-long Ozark Highlands National Recreation Trail runs through the campground, and it is a pleasure to hike. You can stroll along the trail just a short distance from the campground and see a good example of the varied Ozark Highlands topography and vegetation. Backpackers hike east to the Hurricane Creek Wilderness or west along the hollows and ridges of the highlands.

The Ozark Mountains are actually an eroded plateau that was uplifted millions of years ago. The southern section is predominantly sandstone, while the northern section, around the Buffalo River, is mostly limestone.

The byway winds south through Ozone and Lynwood and ends at the national forest boundary north of Clarksville. Pleasant Hill Ranger Station is just north of Clarksville and has information on the national forest. The Walton Fine Arts Center has exhibits and shows at the University of the Ozarks, also in Clarksville. Nearby, Dardanelle Reservoir impounds the Arkansas River and offers fishing, boating, camping, and swimming.

37

Pig Trail Scenic Byway
Ozark National Forest

General description: A 19-mile route that meanders through the scenic Boston Mountains.

Special attractions: Colorful autumn foliage, canoeing, fishing, hunting, Ozark Highlands Trail, camping, spring wildflowers, spectacular panoramic views.

Location: Western Arkansas on the Ozark National Forest, northeast of Fort Smith, The byway follows Arkansas Route 23 on national forest land between Brashears and Ozark.

Byway route number: Arkansas Route 23.

Travel season: Year-round.

Camping: One national forest campground near the byway, with picnic tables, toilets, fire grates, and drinking water. No hookups.

Services: Small store, gas, and canoe rental at Turners Bend. All services in nearby Ozark and Fayetteville.

Nearby attractions: Fort Smith Historical Site, White Rock Mountain Recreation Area, Arkansas River and Ozark Lake, War Eagle Craft Fair, Shores Lake, and Ozark Highlands, Arkansas Highway 7, and Mount Magazine national forest scenic byways.

For more information: See the appendix for contact information.

 The Drive

The Pig Trail Scenic Byway crosses the Boston Mountains in the Ozark Highlands, offering far-ranging views of the heavily forested, rolling landscape. The two-lane road is paved and has turnouts for scenic and recreation access. It is a major thoroughfare, and traffic is moderately heavy in spring, summer, and fall. It is lighter in winter.

Summer temperatures range from the 60s at night to the 80s and 90s during the day. Spring and autumn range from the 50s to the 80s, and winter days reach the 40s, with temperatures dropping below freezing at night.

This byway was given its unusual name for several reasons. It winds and meanders through the mountains much as a game or wild-pig trail does, and it is the route traveled by many of the fans who attend the University of Arkansas' Razorbacks football games. If you drive this byway on an autumn

Drive 37: Pig Trail Scenic Byway
Ozark National Forest

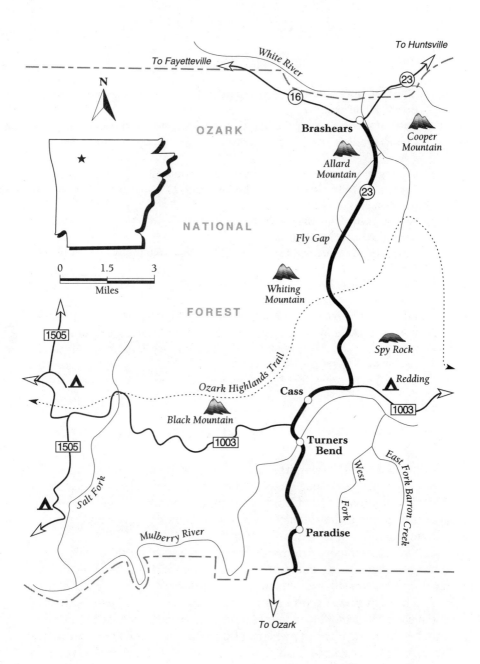

The Pig Trail Scenic Byway winds along a stream and travels through hardwood forests and pasturelands in the Boston Mountains. Ozark National Forest photo

weekend, you may encounter carloads of people wearing bright-red hog hats and yelling "wooo-pig-sooee" out the windows as they drive by.

If you plan to travel the byway from north to south, you begin at the national forest boundary at Brashears. Canoeing, kayaking, and fishing are popular on the nearby White River. The byway winds alongside a sparkling stream, part of the headwaters of the White River, and climbs Allard Mountain. The region is forested with a mixture of oaks and hickories, as well as smaller stands of pines, cedars, and hardwoods. Autumn colors are spectacular, and spring blossoms are equally splendid.

Drive south through Fly Gap, the highest spot on the Pig Trail at an elevation of 1,953 feet. South of Fly Gap, the 165-mile-long Ozark Highlands Trail crosses the byway at Cherry Bend, near milepost 37 on the highway. This National Scenic Trail is an east-west trending footpath across the entire Boston Range. It begins at Lake Fort Smith State Park on the western end of the national forest and goes out the northeastern edge of the forest to the Buffalo National River. You may wish to walk a portion of it. The trail is steep east of the byway, and it leads to Cherry Bend Hollow and broad vistas. West of the byway, the trail is fairly easy and goes around the mountain. About 0.25-mile west of the byway, the ruins of an old rock house lie under the bluff near the trail.

The byway continues south across the rolling ridges and hills of the highlands, and the views are different at each bend in the road. The Mulberry River drainage, mountains, and the hardwood overstory are visible from byway viewpoints.

A side trip 3 miles east on Forest Road 1003 leads to Redding Campground's 27 sites along the Mulberry River. An 8.5-mile loop trail begins at Redding and climbs to Spy Rock for a wonderful view of the Mulberry River Valley. The foot trail also intersects the Ozark Highlands Trail. Anglers fish the Mulberry for smallmouth bass, warm water perches, and catfish.

The community of Cass sits in the deep valley along the Mulberry River, just south of the Forest Road 1003 turnoff. In the 1920s and '30s, the Cass-Combs Railroad used some unusual techniques for getting lumber up to the ridge tops: a windlass lowered empty railcars to the riverside lumber mill, and then oxen pulled the loaded cars up the steep roads to the ridge top. From there, the lumber was hauled by rail to St. Paul or Fayetteville. Also in Cass, the Job Corp Civilian Conservation Center trains more than 200 young people a year in various occupational skills, such as carpentry, plumbing, masonry, painting, and heavy-equipment operation. Visitors may tour the facilities, or stop for information on the Ozark National Forest.

The byway crosses the Mulberry River, which is navigable between mid-March and early June and again in late fall. The river drops about a foot per mile in elevation and is classified as class III whitewater. You may see canoeists and kayakers negotiating the whitewater where the byway crosses the river. Just beyond the river crossing, a side trip west on Forest Road 1003 will lead to several campgrounds.

Turners Bend has a small store and rents canoes. Farther south, the byway ascends Bend Hill through pines and cedars and past picturesque old homesteads with barns and stone fences. It continues through Paradise and ends at the national forest boundary north of Ozark.

The Boston Ranger Station in Ozark has visitor information about the national forest. Nearby, the Arkansas River provides numerous recreational opportunities, such as fishing, waterskiing, and boating.

38

Mount Magazine Scenic Byway
Ozark National Forest

General description: A 24.9-mile drive through hardwood forests to the top of Mount Magazine.

Special attractions: Colorful autumn foliage, high sandstone bluffs, spring blossoms, camping, extensive views of mountain and pastures.

Location: Northwest Arkansas on the Ozark National Forest, southeast of Fort Smith. The byway follows Arkansas Route 309 between Paris and Havana and includes spur roads into the Mount Magazine Recreation Area.

Byway route numbers: Arkansas Route 309, Forest Road 1606, Forest Road 1636, and Forest Road 1606A.

Travel season: Year-round.

Camping: Two national forest campgrounds with picnic tables, drinking water, fire grates, and toilets. No hookups.

Services: No services on the byway. All services in nearby Paris and Havana.

Nearby attractions: Blue Mountain Lake, Dardanelle Reservoir, numerous local festivals, Logan County Museum in Paris, historic city of Fort Smith, winery tours, Spring Lake Recreation Area, and Pig Trail, Ozark Highlands, and Arkansas Highway 7 national forest scenic byways.

For more information: See the appendix for contact information.

 The Drive

The Mount Magazine Scenic Byway climbs from the Arkansas River Valley up to flat-topped Mount Magazine and then winds down to the Petit Jean River Valley. The two-lane road is paved and has turnouts for scenic and recreational opportunities. Traffic is steady on weekends and light on weekdays.

Summers are hot and humid, with temperatures averaging in the 90s and sometimes exceeding 100 degrees. The top of the mountain averages 10 to 15 degrees cooler than the surrounding valleys. The region gets about 45 inches of rain a year. July through September is generally dry, and the rains begin in October. Autumn and spring are pleasant, with daytime temperatures in the 60s. Winter days reach the 40s, with freezing weather common at night in January and February.

Drive 38: Mount Magazine Scenic Byway
Ozark National Forest

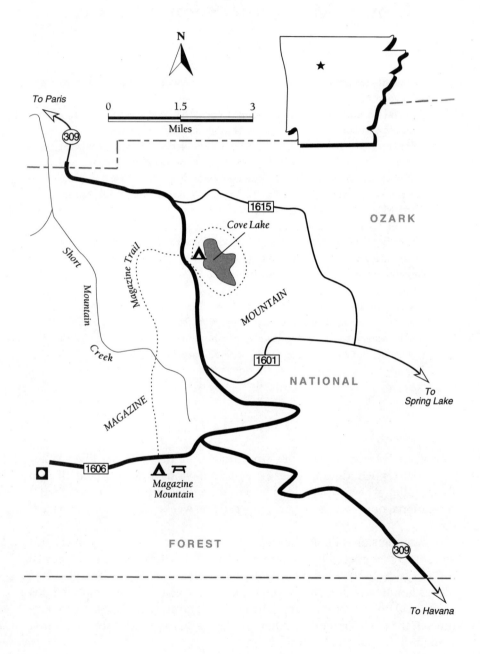

N

To Paris

309

0   1.5   3
Miles

OZARK

1615

Cove Lake

Short Mountain Creek

Magazine Trail

MOUNTAIN

1601

NATIONAL

To
Spring Lake

MAGAZINE

1606

Magazine
Mountain

FOREST

309

To Havana

To drive the byway from north to south, begin in Paris, where the Magazine Ranger Station has national forest information. The byway starts at the national forest boundary just south of Paris and immediately starts to climb.

The forest is composed primarily of shortleaf pines, with mixed stands of red and white oaks, hickories, gums, and maples. The lush understory includes wild plums, wild roses, mulberries, and spicebushes, as well as Osage oranges, sassafras, and edible berries such as huckleberries, black-berries, dewberries, and gooseberries. The forest is spectacular when the leaves have turned color, from late October through early November. In the spring, blossoming shrubs and trees are also lovely.

The first campground is located at 160-acre Cove Lake Recreation Area. There are 28 campsites, restrooms, and showers in the summer. Additionally, Cove Lake has picnicking, swimming, fishing, a hiking trail, and a boat-launch ramp. Anglers fish for largemouth bass, catfish, and bream. The hiking trail encircles Cove Lake in a 3-mile loop, with a spur to a vista point. Another trail leads to an old CCC campsite.

The byway climbs through scattered private land and farms. Logging, grazing, wildlife management, and watershed protection are activities that are promoted in the national forest. The USDA Forest Service maintains

Rock formations and bluffs await visitors to the Mount Magazine Scenic Byway.
Ozark National Forest photo

picnic areas and scenic overlooks on the byway, which allow views north over the forest to the Arkansas River Valley, and south over the Petit Jean River Valley.

Wildflowers are abundant and varied, both along the roadside and in the forest. Spring beauties, Johnny-jump-ups, jack-in-the-pulpits, and violets bloom each spring, and summer blossoms include May apples, columbines, and many varieties of orchids and lilies. Autumn flowers are predominantly asters and sunflowers.

The byway climbs and turns onto the national forest spur roads that lead into the Mount Magazine Recreation Area. Here you will find three picnic areas, numerous vista points, hiking trails, and a campground. The campground has 13 sites in the forest on the mountaintop. Signal Hill Trail is a short route to the very top of Mount Magazine. East End Trail goes from the campground through the woods to East End Picnic Area. The Magazine Trail leaves Mount Magazine Recreation Area and parallels the west side of the byway 10.8 miles down to Cove Lake. This footpath through young and old stands of hardwoods and pines is moderately difficult, but it offers beautiful views along the way.

Mount Magazine, at 2,753 feet in elevation, is the highest mountain in Arkansas. It is about 7 miles long and 3 miles wide, and it dominates the landscape. Views from the flat top on a clear day can extend 50 miles and can include Blue Mountain Lake in the Petit Jean River Valley, Dardanelle Reservoir in the Arkansas River Valley, high sandstone bluffs and cliffs, and dense forests and pastures on the rolling hills that surround the mountain. The mountain is primarily sandstone and shale, uplifted along with the Arkansas River millions of years ago.

Back on Arkansas Route 309, the byway descends the south side of Mount Magazine, again offering extensive views. The road winds and twists down the mountain and through the pine and hardwood forest. Forest inhabitants include raccoons, deer, foxes, black bears, bobcats, opossums, skunks, and squirrels. Songbirds are plentiful and include indigo buntings, purple martins, whip-poor-wills, mockingbirds, and cardinals. Seeing painted buntings, scarlet and summer tanagers, and rufous-crowned sparrows would be a rare treat. Naturalists are interested in the threatened Mount Magazine middle-toothed land snail and the maple-leafed oak tree. Both are found only on Mount Magazine.

The byway ends at the national forest boundary north of Havana.

39

Arkansas Highway 7 Scenic Byway

Ozark and Ouachita National Forests

General description: Two sections of highway, totaling 60.6 miles, through the Ouachita Mountains and the Boston Mountains in the Ozark Highlands.

Special attractions: Brilliant autumn foliage, spring wildflowers, Ozark Highlands and Ouachita national recreation trails, Rotary Ann Overlook.

Location: West-central Arkansas on the Ozark and Ouachita national forests, east of Fort Smith. One section of the byway follows Arkansas Route 7 north of Hot Springs National Park, on national forest lands between Jessieville and Fourche Junction. The other section travels Arkansas Route 7 north of Russellville, on national forest lands between Dover and Jasper.

Byway route number: Arkansas Route 7.

Travel season: Year-round.

Camping: Four national forest campgrounds with picnic tables, drinking water, fire grates, and toilets. No hookups.

Services: Scattered limited services along the byway. All services in nearby Hot Springs National Park, Russellville, and Harrison.

Nearby attractions: Alum Cove Natural Bridge and Interpretive Trail; Pedestal Rocks; Sam's Throne; Buffalo National River; Dardanelle Reservoir; Big Piney, Richland, and Hurricane creeks; Hot Springs National Park; Lake Ouachita State Park; Ozark Highlands, Pig Trail, Mount Magazine, and Talimena national forest scenic byways; and Hurricane Creek, Richland Creek, Upper Buffalo, and East Fork wilderness areas.

For more information: See the appendix for contact information.

 The Drive

The Arkansas Highway 7 Scenic Byway is actually two separate sections of the same north-south highway. The section through the Ouachita National Forest is 24.3 miles long, and the section in the Ozark National Forest totals 36.3 miles. The byway segments are separated by about 40 miles of the populated Arkansas River Valley. The winding two-lane highway is paved and has turnouts for scenic and recreational access.

Summers are generally hot, with daytime temperatures in the 80s and

Drive 39: Arkansas Highway 7 Scenic Byway
Ozark and Ouachita National Forests

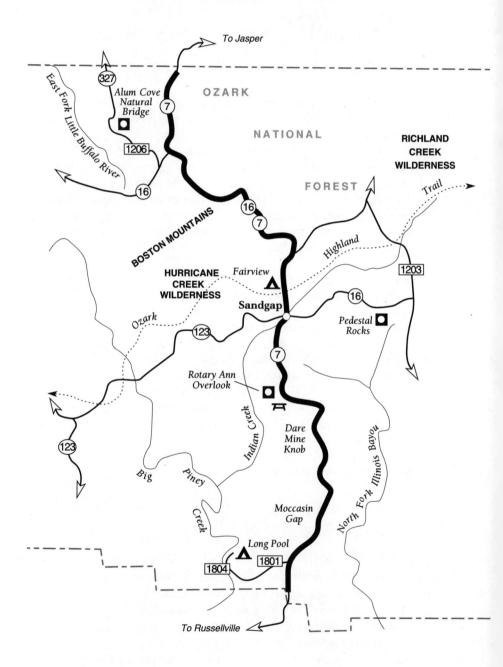

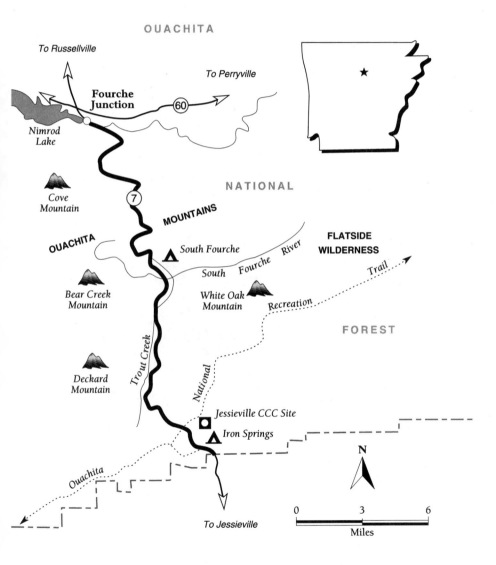

OUACHITA

To Russellville

To Perryville

Fourche Junction

60

Nimrod Lake

NATIONAL

Cove Mountain

7

MOUNTAINS

South Fourche

South   Fourche   River

FLATSIDE WILDERNESS

Trail

OUACHITA

Bear Creek Mountain

White Oak Mountain

Recreation

FOREST

Trout Creek

Deckard Mountain

National

Jessieville CCC Site

Iron Springs

N

Ouachita

0   3   6

To Jessieville

Miles

90s and evenings somewhat cooler. Spring and autumn range from the mid-50s to 80s, and winter days often reach the 50s and 60s, with freezing nights and ice or sleet in January and February, especially on the northern portion of the byway.

Beginning at the north and traveling south, enter the byway at the national forest boundary south of Jasper. The Buffalo Ranger Station in Jasper has information about the national forest, the byway, and the nearby Buffalo National River, which winds through high limestone bluffs and is popular for fishing and for white-water kayaking and canoeing in springtime.

The byway heads south alongside Henderson Mountain. A side trip west on Arkansas Route 16 and Forest Road 1206 leads 5 miles to Alum Cove Natural Bridge Recreation Area. There are picnic tables, restrooms, drinking water, and a 1-mile interpretive nature trail. Walkers see the caves and rock formations along the bluffs and stroll through stands of American beeches, umbrella magnolias, and dogwoods. The natural bridge is 130 feet long and 20 feet wide, and it was carved by the erosive action of wind and water.

Back on the byway, continue south, gaining elevation and rolling through the hardwood forest. Fairview Campground has 11 sites on a small

Arkansas Highway 7 Scenic Byway meanders through the lovely hardwood forests in the Ouachita and Boston mountain ranges. OZARK NATIONAL FOREST PHOTO

hill above the highway. The dogwoods and redbuds are beautiful in spring.

The Ozark Highlands Trail crosses the byway at Fairview Campground. This 165-mile national recreation trail follows clear streams and ascends mountains on its scenic east-west route. You can hike a portion of it from the campground; the trail goes about 5 miles west to the Hurricane Creek Wilderness Area or about 17 miles east through Richland Creek Wilderness to Richland Creek Campground. Hurricane Creek Wilderness encompasses 15,427 acres of upland southern hardwoods, as well as flat-topped mountains and limestone bluffs. Richland Creek Wilderness has 11,801 acres of slightly steeper terrain and higher elevations.

Continue south on Arkansas Route 7. Tiny Sandgap lies about midway through this section of the byway. Here, a side trip east on Arkansas Route 16 leads 5 miles to unique pedestal rock formations carved into the bluff.

Back on the byway, the route goes south through Piney Creeks Wildlife Management Area. This area is inhabited by big and small game species, notably white-tailed deer, turkeys, and black bears. Ruffed grouse were recently reintroduced to the area.

The highway climbs to the popular Rotary Ann Overlook and Picnic Area. This popular overlook allows a splendid view of forests and mountains.

The route crosses rolling terrain past Freeman Springs and Dare Mine Knob and through Moccasin Gap before dropping down to its end at the national forest boundary. A side trip just before the boundary, west on Forest Road 1801 and Forest Road 1804, leads to Long Pool Recreation Area on Big Piney Creek. Long Pool has 19 campsites, picnicking, a swimming beach, and canoe access. Large, natural pools make great swimming holes under the high bluffs. Anglers fish for smallmouth, largemouth, and spotted bass, along with several species of sunfish. Floaters enjoy seasonal canoeing and kayaking in the creek.

The northern end of the second part of the byway is at the community of Fourche Junction on Nimrod Lake. Nimrod has boating and fishing opportunities.

From the junction, drive south on the winding road through the Ouachita National Forest. "Ouachita" is the French phonetic spelling for an Indian word that means good hunting grounds. The well-known Ouachita whetstones and quartz crystals come from this area. The Ouachita Forest hosts white-tailed deer, wild turkeys, beavers, squirrels, rabbits, raccoons, quail, turtles, and various waterfowl such as great blue herons, egrets, and wood ducks. Canada geese and mallards pass through during migration.

This southern section of the byway crosses through a dense forest of shortleaf pines and occasional stands of hardwoods. The Ouachita Mountains are unique in being an east-west trending range. Most ranges in North America trend north and south.

About midway through this section of the byway is South Fourche Campground, with seven roadside campsites near South Fourche Creek. Anglers try for brown perch, bass, and catfish in the creek. Nights spent camping in Arkansas are filled with the sounds of frogs, toads, locusts, owls, and whip-poor-wills. The songs of birds brighten mornings.

Continuing south, the byway ascends beside Trace Creek, a pretty stream that sparkles and murmurs under the forest canopy. There are abundant and beautiful wildflowers along the byway and in the adjacent forest. They include lilies, columbines, orchids, crested irises, and asters. The 8,200-acre Deckard Mountain Walk-In Turkey Hunting Area is west of the byway.

Ouachita National Recreation Trail crosses the byway 1 mile north of Iron Springs Campground. This footpath is 192 miles long and runs east to west from Pinnacle Mountain State Park, through the Ouachita National Forest, to Talimena State Park in Oklahoma. West of the byway, the 4- to 5-mile-long loop known as Hunt's Loop Trail connects with the Ouachita Trail and Iron Springs Recreation Area. Hikers can reach the Ouachita Trail and Hunt's Loop Trail from the byway or from Iron Springs Recreation Area. The loop is moderately difficult and best hiked in a counterclockwise direction. There is a spectacular view south from the rocky bluff atop Short Mountain.

Iron Springs Campground has 13 sites in the woods near a spring and stream. A pleasant wading area and a picnic shelter are available.

The byway ends at the national forest boundary near Jessieville. The ranger station in Jessieville has a visitor information center. Travelers continuing south reach Lake Ouachita and Hot Springs National Park.

40

Talimena Scenic Byway
Ouachita National Forest

General description: A 54-mile winding highway atop the crest of the Ouachita Mountains.

Special attractions: Robert S. Kerr Memorial Arboretum and Nature Center, Queen Wilhelmina State Park and Lodge, historical sites, far-ranging views, camping.

Location: The border between east-central Oklahoma and west-central Arkansas, on the Ouachita National Forest. The byway follows Oklahoma Route 1 and Arkansas Route 88 from the national forest boundary just north of Talihina, Oklahoma, to the community of Mena, Arkansas.

Byway route numbers: Oklahoma Route 1 and Arkansas Route 88.

Travel season: Year-round. The highway is occasionally closed because of snow, and winter driving conditions may be hazardous.

Camping: One national forest campground with picnic tables, flush toilets, fire rings, and drinking water. One state park campground with picnic tables, fire grates, electric and water hookups, bathhouse, laundry, and trailer dumping station. Open April through mid-November.

Services: No services on the byway, but all services available in Talihina and Mena.

Nearby attractions: Black Fork Mountain and Upper Kiamichi wilderness areas, Broken Bow Reservoir, Cedar Lake Recreation Area.

For more information: See the appendix for contact information.

 The Drive

The Talimena Scenic Byway crosses the Ouachita Mountains, the highest range between the Appalachians and the Rockies. The byway route varies in elevation from 1,150 to 2,681 feet as it travels the crest of Rich Mountain and Winding Stair Mountain. The two-lane highway is paved and has frequent turnouts for scenic and recreational access. There are some steep grades and sharp curves.

The average summer temperature in this area is about 80 degrees. Spring and fall have moderate temperatures, and the haze of summer humidity is generally blown away by thunderstorms. Winters average 43 degrees, with occasional light snowfalls. Temperatures dip below freezing at night, and

Drive 40: Talimena Scenic Byway
Ouachita National Forest

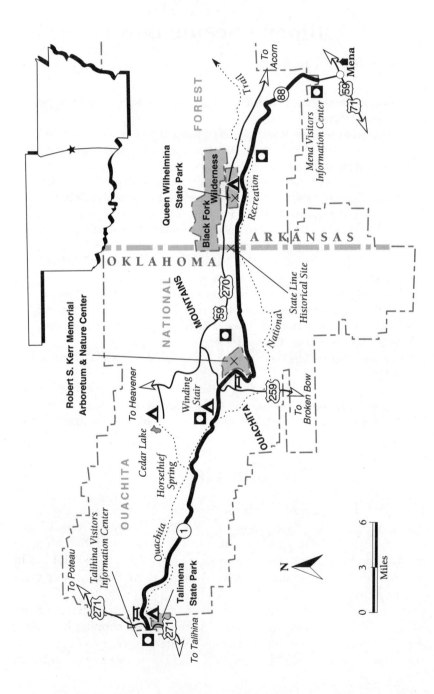

the wind blows constantly. Tornadoes occur periodically.

The byway can be driven from either direction or entered at about its midpoint via U.S. Highway 259. It is named for the two communities at either end: Talihina and Mena.

Driving from west to east, the Talimena Scenic Byway begins about 6 miles northeast of Talihina, Oklahoma. Talihina was a missionary settlement established in 1888 and named for the Choctaw Indian word for iron road, meaning the railroad. Talimena State Park, near the byway entrance, has 40 campsites, picnic tables, toilets, and some hookups. Talihina Visitor Center, at the beginning of the byway, has displays, exhibits, and information about the area. Nearby, picnicking is pleasant at Old Military Road Picnic Area.

The byway heads east on Oklahoma Route 1 on the Ouachita National Forest. Ouachita takes its name from the Choctaw Indian word "Owachita," which means hunting trip.

The mountains run east and west rather than north and south. They are primarily composed of sandstone and shale of the Mississippi and Pennsylvanian formations, thrust upward with tight folding and faulting. Many of the faults are visible from the byway.

The byway climbs Winding Stair Mountain. Ouachita National Recreation Trail parallels the highway, and there are a number of access points for hiking portions of the trail. The trail tends to rough and quite steep in places.

About 16 miles from the beginning of the byway is Horsethief Spring, a historic site. In the 1830s, the Fort Towson Trail, a much-used military road, crossed this site. It was also the probable stopover for many a horse thief en route from stealing horses in Arkansas and driving them to Texas to sell. You can picnic here or hike 4 miles to 84-acre Cedar Lake, which has camping, showers, boating, picnicking, and hiking and nature trails.

Emerald Vista Picnic Area offers views of the scenic byway, the Poteau River Valley, Cedar Lake, and Lake Wister. Winding Stair Campground has 26 campsites in the forest.

About midway through the scenic byway, the road crosses U.S. Highway 259 and continues east on Oklahoma Route 1. Robert S. Kerr Memorial Arboretum and Nature Center is a few miles past the intersection. Named for the late senator from Oklahoma, the center has three interpretive trails, each less than 1 mile in length. One focuses on soil formation, another identifies various plants and trees, and the third explains plant succession and communities. The arboretum and nature center is a delightful place to spend a few hours or a whole day. The experience offered there is both interesting and challenging.

The byway area is home to a great variety of birds, including warblers, grosbeaks, vireos, finches, and owls. Mammals include white-tailed deer, opossums, raccoons, foxes, bobcats, skunks, and squirrels.

The forest is composed of a variety of tree species. The north slopes and ridge tops are covered mostly with oaks, gums, hickories, elms, maples, cherry trees, and black walnuts. The south slopes have shortleaf pines and mixed hardwoods, as well as flowering shrubs such as dogwoods and redbuds. Spring is lovely along the byway, with the blossoming shrubs and wildflowers creating a colorful display. Autumn brings a photographer's and sightseer's dream; the palette of bright colors reaches from the underbrush to the tops of the trees.

The byway goes east to the Oklahoma-Arkansas state line and continues on as Arkansas Route 88. Queen Wilhemina State Park lies a few miles east of the state line atop Rich Mountain. Views of the surrounding mountains are extensive. There is a lodge, restaurant, activities, store, summer visitor center, amphitheater, hiking trails, and naturalist programs. The campground has 40 sites, a bathhouse, laundry, trailer dumping station, and hookups.

Rich Mountain Lookout is the highest point on the byway, at elevation 2,681 feet. You can picnic here, and the breathtaking view includes Queen Wilhemina State Park, Black Fork Mountain Wilderness Area, and the Mill Creek area.

The highway descends Rich Mountain, and there are frequent scenic overlooks. The byway ends at Mena Visitor Information Station, at the national forest boundary.

The Talimena Scenic Byway offers far-ranging views as it winds along the crest of the Ouachita Mountains. OUACHITA NATIONAL FOREST PHOTO

Appendix: Contact Information

Drive 1: Scenic Highway

Chippewa National Forest, Route 3, Box 244, Cass Lake, MN 56633, 218-335-8600.
  Blackduck Ranger District, HC 3, Box 95, Blackduck, MN 56630, 218-835-4291.
  Cass Lake Ranger District, Route 3, Box 219, Cass Lake, MN 56633, 218-335-2283.

Drive 2: Avenue of Pines Scenic Byway

Chippewa National Forest, Route 3, Box 244, Cass Lake, MN 56633, 218-335-8600.
  Deer River Ranger District, P.O. Box 308, Deer River, MN 56636, 218-246-2123.

Drive 3: Edge of the Wilderness Scenic Byway

Chippewa National Forest, Route 3 Box 244, Cass Lake, MN 56633, 218-335-8600.
Marcell Ranger District, Marcell, MN 56657, 218-832-3161.

Drive 4: North Shore Drive

Superior National Forest, 8901 Grand Avenue Place, Duluth, MN 55808-1102, 218-626-4300.
  Tofte Ranger District, Tofte, MN 55615, 218-663-8063.
  Gunflint Ranger District, P.O. Box 790, Grand Marais, MN 55604, 218-387-3200.

Drive 5: Great Divide Highway

Chequamegon National Forest, 1170 Fourth Avenue South, Park Falls, WI 54552, 715-762-2461.
  Great Divide Ranger District, P.O. Box 126, Glidden, WI 54527, 713-264-2511 and at
  P.O. Box 896, Hayward, WI 54843, 715-634-4821.

Drive 6: Heritage Drive

Nicolet National Forest, 68 South Stevens Street, Rhinelander, WI 54501, 715-362-1300.
  Eagle River Ranger District, P.O. Box 1809, Eagle River, WI 54521, 715-479-2827.

Drive 7: Black River Scenic Byway

Ottawa National Forest, East 6248 U.S. Highway 2, Ironwood, MI 49938, 906-932-1330.
  Bessemer Ranger District, 500 North Moore Street, Bessemer, MI 49911-1096; 906-667-0261.

Drive 8: Whitefish Bay Scenic Byway

Hiawatha National Forest, 2727 North Lincoln Road, Escanaba, MI 49829, 906-786-4062.
  Sault Ste. Marie Ranger District, 4000 Interstate 75 Business Spur, Sault Ste. Marie, MI 49783, 906-635-5311.

Drive 9: River Road

Huron-Manistee National Forests, 1755 South Mitchell Street, Cadillac, MI 49601, 800-821-6263.
 Huron Shores Ranger District, 5761 North Skeel Avenue, Oscoda, MI 48750, 517-739-0728.

Drive 10: Ohio River Scenic Byway

Hoosier National Forest, 811 Constitution Avenue, Bedford, IN 47421, 812-275-5987.
 Tell City Ranger District, 248 Fifteenth Street, Tell City, IN 47586, 812-547-7051.
Harrison-Crawford State Forest and Wyandotte State Recreation Area, 7240 Old Forest Road SW, Corydon, IN 47112, 812-738-8232.
 Wyandotte Caves, Rural Route 1 Box 85, Leavenworth, IN 47137, 812-738-2782.

Drive 11: Shawnee Hills on the Ohio Scenic Byway

Shawnee National Forest, 50 Highway 145 South, Harrisburg, IL 62946, 618-253-7114.
 Elizabethtown Ranger District, Route 2 Box 4, Elizabethtown, IL 62931, 618-287-2201.
 Vienna Ranger District, Route 1 Box 288B, Vienna, IL 62995, 618-658-2111.

Drive 12: Sugar Camp Scenic Byway

Mark Twain National Forest, 401 Fairgrounds Road, Rolla, MO 65401, 573-364-4621.
 Cassville Ranger District, Highway 248 East (P.O. Box 310), Cassville, MO 65625, 417-847-2144.

Drive 13: Glade Top Trail

Mark Twain National Forest, 401 Fairgrounds Road, Rolla, MO 65401, 314-364-4621.
 Ava Ranger District, 1103 South Jefferson, Ava, MO 65608, 417-683-4428.

Drive 14: Blue Buck Knob Scenic Byway

Mark Twain National Forest, 401 Fairgrounds Road, Rolla, MO 65401, 573-364-4621.
 Willow Springs Ranger District, P.O. Box 99, Willow Springs, MO 65793, 417-469-3155.

Drive 15: Covered Bridge Scenic Byway

Wayne National Forest, 219 Columbus Road, Athens, OH 45701, 740-592-6644.
 Athens Ranger District, Marietta Unit, Route 1 Box 132, Marietta, OH 45750, 740-373-9055.

Drive 16: Highland Scenic Byway

Monongahela National Forest, 200 Sycamore Street, Elkins, WV 26241, 304-636-1800.
 Gauley Ranger District, P.O. Box 110, Richwood, WV 26261, 304-846-2695.
 Marlinton Ranger District, P.O. Box 210, Marlinton, WV 24954, 304-799-4334.
Weekends:
Cranberry Mountain Nature Center, 304-653-4826.

Drive 17: Longhouse Scenic Byway

Allegheny National Forest, 222 Liberty Street P.O. Box 847), Warren, PA 16365, 814-723-5150.
Bradford Ranger District, Star Route 1 Box 88, Bradford, PA 16701, 814-362-4613.

Drive 18: Kancamagus Scenic Byway

White Mountain National Forest, 719 North Main Street, Laconia, NH 03246, 603-528-8721.
Pemigewasset Ranger District, RFD 3 Box 15, Plymouth, NH 03264, 603-536-1310.
Saco Ranger District, 33 Kancamagus Highway, Conway, NH 03818, 603-447-5448.
Call 800-280-CAMP for campground reservations.

Drive 19: Highlands Scenic Tour

George Washington National Forest, 5162 Valley Point Parkway, Roanoke, VA 24019, 540-265-5100 or 888-265-0019.
James River Ranger District, 810A Madison Avenue, Covington, VA 24426, 540-962-2214.

Drive 20: Big Walker Mountain Scenic Byway

Jefferson National Forest, 5162 Valley Point Parkway, Roanoke, VA 24019, 540-265-5100 or 888-265-0019.
Wytheville Ranger District, 155 Sherwood Forest Road, Wytheville, VA 24382, 540-228-5551.

Drive 21: Mount Rogers Scenic Byway

Jefferson National Forest, 5162 Valley Point Parkway, Roanoke, VA 24019, 540-265-5100 or 888-265-0019.

Mount Rogers National Recreation Area, 3714 Highway 16, Marion, VA 24354, 540-783-5196.

Drive 22: Zilpo Road

Daniel Boone National Forest, 1700 Bypass, Winchester, KY 40391, 606-745-3100.
Morehead Ranger District, 2375 Kentucky 801 South, Morehead, KY 40351, 606-784-6429.

Drive 23: Ocoee Scenic Byway

Cherokee National Forest, 2800 North Ocoee Street, P.O. Box 2010, Cleveland, TN 37320, 423-476-9700.
Ocoee Ranger District, Route 1 Box 348D, Benton, TN 37307, 423-338-5201.

Drive 24: Overhill Skyway

Cherokee National Forest, 2800 North Ocoee Street, P.O. Box 2010, Cleveland, TN 37320, 423-476-9700.
Tellico Ranger District, 250 Ranger Station Road, Tellico Plains, TN 37385, 423-253-2520.

Nantahala National Forest, National Forests in North Carolina, P.O. Box 2750, Asheville, NC 28802; 828-257-4200.
Cheoah Ranger Station, Rte. 1 Box 16-A, Robbinsville, NC 28771, 828-479-6431.

Tennessee Overhill Heritage Association, P.O. Box 143, Etowah, TN 37331, 423-263-7232.

Drive 25: Mountain Waters Scenic Byway

National Forests in North Carolina, P.O. Box 2750, Asheville, NC 28802, 828-257-4200.
Highlands Ranger District, 2010 Flat Mountain Road, Highlands, NC 28741, 828-526-3765.
Wayah Ranger District, 90 Sloan Road, Franklin, NC 28734, 828-524-6441.

Drive 26: Forest Heritage Scenic Byway

National Forests in North Carolina, P.O. Box 2750, Asheville, NC 28802, 704-257-4200.
Pisgah Ranger District, 1001 Pisgah Highway, Pisgah Forest, NC 28768, 704-877-3265.

Drive 27: Oscar Wiggington Memorial Scenic Byway

Sumter National Forest, 4931 Broad River Road, Columbia, SC 29212-3530, 803-561-4000.
Andrew Pickens Ranger District, 112 Andrew Pickens Circle, Mountain Rest, SC 29664, 864-638-9568.

Oconee State Park, 624 State Park Road, Mountain Rest, SC 29664, 864-638-5353.

Drive 28: Ridge and Valley Scenic Byway

Chattahoochee National Forest, 775 Cleveland Highway, Gainesville, GA 30501, 770-536-0541.
Armuchee Ranger District, 806 East Villanow, P.O. Box 465, LaFayette, GA 30728, 706-638-1085.

Drive 29: Russell-Brasstown Scenic Byway

Chattahoochee National Forest, 775 Cleveland Highway, Gainesville, GA 30501, 770-536-0541.
Brasstown Ranger District, P.O. Box 9, 1881 Highway 515, Blairsville, GA 30514, 706-745-6928.
Chattooga Ranger District, P.O. Box 196, Highway 197, North Burton Rd., Clarkesville, GA 30523, 706-754-6221.

Drive 30: Apalachee Savannahs Scenic Byway

National Forests in Florida, Woodcrest Office Park, 325 John Knox Road, Suite F100, Tallahassee, FL 32303, 850-942-9300.
Apalachicola Ranger District, Highway 20, P.O. Box 579, Bristol, FL 32321, 850-643-2282.

Drive 31: Talladega Scenic Drive

National Forests of Alabama, 2946 Chestnut Street, Montgomery, AL 36107, 334-832-4470.
> *Talladega Ranger District,* 1001 North Street Highway 21 North), Talladega, AL 35160, 205-362-2909.
> *Shoal Creek Ranger District,* 450 Highway 46, Heflin, AL 36264, 205-463-2272.

Cheaha State Park, 2141 Bunker Loop, Delta, AL 36258, 256-488-5115 or 800-252-7275.

Drive 32: Natchez Trace Scenic Byway

National Forests in Mississippi, 100 West Capitol Street, Suite 1141, Federal Building, Jackson, MS 39269, 601-960-4391.
> *Tombigbee Ranger District,* Route 1 Box 98A, Ackerman, MS 39735, 601-285-3264.

Drive 33: Longleaf Trail Scenic Byway

Kisatchie National Forest, P.O. Box 5500, 2500 Shreveport Highway, Pineville, LA 71360, 318-473-7160.
> *Kisatchie Ranger District,* P.O. Box 2128, Natchitoches, LA 71457, 318-352-2568.

Drive 34: St. Francis Scenic Byway

Ozark–St. Francis National Forests, P.O. Box 1008, 605 W. Main, Russellville, AR 72801, 501-968-2354.
> *St. Francis Ranger District,* 2675 Highway 44, Marianna, AR 72360, 870-295-5278.

Drive 35: Sylamore Scenic Byway

Ozark–St. Francis National Forests, P.O. Box 1008, 605 West Main, Russellville, AR 72801, 501-968-2354.
> *Sylamore Ranger District,* P.O. Box 1279, Highway 14 North, Mountain View, AR 72560, 870-269-3228.

Blanchard Visitor Information Center, 870-757-2211.

Drive 36: Ozark Highlands Scenic Byway

Ozark–St. Francis National Forests, P.O. Box 1008, 605 West Main, Russellville, AR 72801, 501-968-2354.
> *Pleasant Hill Ranger District,* P.O. Box 190, Highway 21 North, Clarksville, AR 72830, 501-754-2864.

Drive 37: Pig Trail Scenic Byway

Ozark–St. Francis National Forests, P.O. Box 1008, 605 West Main, Russellville, AR 72801, 501-968-2354.
> *Boston Mountain Ranger District,* Highway 23 North, P.O. Box 76, Ozark, AR 72949, 501-667-2191.

Drive 38: Mount Magazine Scenic Byway

Ozark–St. Francis National Forests, P.O. Box 1008, 605 West Main, Russellville, AR 72801, 501-968-2354.

    Magazine Ranger District, P.O. Box 511, 3001 East Walnut, Paris, AR 72855, 501-963-3076.

Drive 39: Arkansas Highway 7 Scenic Byway

Ouachita National Forest, P.O. Box 1270, Hot Springs National Park, AR 71902, 501-321-5202.

    Ozark–St. Francis National Forests, P.O. Box 1008, 605 West Main, Russellville, AR 72801, 501-968-2354.

    Buffalo Ranger District, P.O. Box 427, Highway 7N, Jasper, AR 72641, 501-446-5122.

    Bayou Ranger District, 12000 SR 27, Hector, AR 72843, 501-284-3150.

    Jessieville Ranger District, P.O Box 189, 8607 Highway 7 North, Jessieville, AR 71949, 501-984-5313.

Drive 40: Talimena Scenic Byway

Ouachita National Forest, P.O. Box 1270, Hot Springs National Park, AR 71902, 501-321-5202.

    Kiamichi Ranger District, P.O. Box 577, Talihina, OK 74571, 918-567-2326.

    Mena Ranger District, 1603 Highway 71N, Mena, AR 71953, 501-394-2382.

    Choctaw Ranger District, HC 64, Box 3467, Heavener, OK 74937, 918-653-2991.

Index

Page numbers appearing in italics refer to maps.

About the Author

Beverly Magley is a freelance writer from Helena, Montana. She is editor of *Montana Magazine* and has written several natural history field guides for children. Ms. Magley is happiest in the outdoors, and she has backpacked, bicycled, rafted, and cross-country skied in such varied locales as the United States, Europe, and the South Pacific.